The Politics of Disorder

THE POLITICS

OF

DISORDER

Theodore J. Lowi

Basic Books, Inc., Publishers

NEW YORK   LONDON

© 1971 by Basic Books, Inc.
Library of Congress Catalog Card Number 74–156941
SBN 465–05965–1
Manufactured in the United States of America

For Mark Lowi

Acknowledgments

Some of these materials were previously published, and I would like to express my gratitude to the University of Chicago Press, *The Nation,* and the American Political Science Association for their permission to reprint. However, publishers as well as readers of the earlier versions may fail to recognize these materials as they now appear because of the very significant work of Professor Charles F. Levine, of the University of Illinois–Chicago Circle Campus. A former student and trusted friend, Professor Levine took on the assignment of editing these materials. He scored great success in Chapters 4 and 5 but due to my recalcitrance was unable to operate as a full-fledged editor on the others. For pushing me to make revisions far beyond my original plans, I am profoundly grateful to Charlie. However, the responsibility for errors in the final product is mine alone.

In so many ways this book is an extension of *The End of Liberalism,* whose critics have been my most useful teachers in the construction of this volume.[1] Among the many whose criticisms have been useful, I wish to single out two colleagues, Norton Long and David Kettler, whose careful reading and energetic goading led me to reconsideration and further explorations that I might not otherwise have undertaken. A large number of students and col-

[1] *The End of Liberalism: Ideology, Policy and the Crisis of Public Authority* (New York: W. W. Norton & Co., Inc., 1969).

leagues were also helpful to me on one chapter or another. These are in no way responsible for the results but I do wish to acknowledge the importance of a few whose efforts were particularly effective: Jo Freeman, Alan Stone, Thomas Blau, and Elliot Feldman, students at the University of Chicago during the course of my work on the book. Other colleagues, whose affiliations are too well established to repeat here, include Professors J. David Barber, Irving Kristol, David Truman, George LaNoue, David Street, Charles Schutz, Robert Paul Wolff, Paul Sheatsley, Paul Oren, and J. David Greenstone. Each had an important impact on one or more chapters.

Finally, I would like to express my gratitude to the students on American and Canadian campuses from MIT to Stanford whose critical attentiveness and hospitality during my visiting lectures helped so much to sharpen my thoughts on the problems of liberalism in an age of crisis. Their questions helped me to identify much more clearly the discontinuities between sociopolitical and governmental processes and led me to iron out the apparent paradox of pluralism which is socially valuable and yet counterproductive when elevated to a principle of government. Their need for explanations caused me to formulate an improved, though far from perfect, theory of how rule-of-law and other formalisms can emerge from actual informal processes. And their distrust of established concepts and institutions goaded me to try, far beyond my abilities, to work out some better relationship between persistence and change, between public and private moralities, between the ends rational discourse can attain and those that action can attain. And just as the skepticism of their youth forced me into fresh considerations, so the arrogance of their inexperience reinforced my dedication to rational discourse and my faith that for educators, education, not politics, is the appropriate calling and the effective technique for social change.

                                                                    TJL

Prologue:
When Institutions Fail

Modern man has a genius for contriving efficient, productive institutions. But inevitably institutions betray him; no institution will ever fulfill all his needs. Best-laid plans simply go astray. Success in one era merely renders institutions incapable of processing adequately the demands of the next era.

When institutions fail, there is disorder—but it is a special kind of disorder. It is not chaos, the disorder of randomness. It does not resemble the disorder of war, revolution, epidemic, craze, or environmental catastrophe. Rather, the failure of institutions brings on a discontent and sense of grievance that leads to large-scale moralizing. People seem to combine alienation with recombination; they seem to reject the collective life when they are actually building another.

When institutions fail, the status quo becomes a calculated risk. Society comes face to face with the choice of waging war on its dilemmas or on those who present the dilemmas. In our own time, a generation after Myrdal's book, America's dilemmas are accepted as the truth, even by those who do not intend to be influenced by the truth.

Every community has its moments of institutional atrophy. In urban history this phenomenon is usually called the "reform cycle," a period of intense revulsion and moralizing following a much longer period of political quiescence. Such reform cycles have occurred much less frequently at the national level because of the vastness of the continent and the complexity of the population— and also because the average level of public morality may have been higher. Still, they *have* occurred nationally, and we seem to have entered such a period now.

Inasmuch as these periods of disorder have been rare in the United States, we in our comfort and affluence have tended to define them as evil times, which must be terminated as quickly as possible, restoring the former state of well-being. The disorder that accompanies the failure of institutions is certainly not comfortable. But it is not merely an obstacle between ourselves and some predetermined paradise. There is a positive side to institutional atrophy. The efficiency of good organization makes things too rigid; tight organization ties people to their established statuses. There has to be some scratching of psychological itches. The weakening of institutions can open up a recycling of opportunities.

This kind of disorder also involves the expansion of political awareness and the intensification of political activity. Political parties are usually pushed out of the picture and are in part replaced by direct political action. Every inconvenience becomes an occasion for political agitation. It is a time for moralizing, a time when people translate their needs into rights. It is a time for clamor that may look like chaos, but only from afar. It is only disorder, the disorder of institutional atrophy.

Ironically, it is also a time when individuals nationalize their perspectives. People toy with new models of behavior. They free themselves from old communities in order to look for new ones. And even though the rhetoric may stress individual rights, local concerns, and local control, all the perspectives are outward. Books that stress individual action and local virtues gain national audiences.

All these characteristics of disorder make the period of institutional atrophy ripe for social movements. In a sense, the social movement is simply the correlative of institutional atrophy. Social movements convert clamor into organizational muscle. This is one of the obvious signs of our having moved into a new era. We can even observe the beginning of a bonafide consumer movement. Student movements have become so intensely moralizing that they appear to be revolutionary. They set such a high moral standard that no person tried can be trusted. Above all, there is in our time the civil rights movement, which, more than anything else, revealed the significant scale of organizational atrophy and maladaptation. The civil rights movement has come to be a congeries of black movements, but this is only owing to the immense frustration presented by the inability of established organizations to be effective. Social movements are providing the kind of focused stress established organizations need before they can adapt themselves.

When moralizing takes the form of social movements, the social structure itself tends to be implicated in one way or another. Each movement tends to reveal the extent to which individual rewards for individual effort are disproportionately allocated, to remind its members and its audiences that established organizations are not living up to their own pretensions. Before our eyes, politics and governments have come unstuck, and there is quite evidently a deep crisis in public authority. Knees are being shaken by still more fundamental changes in human relationships. To face these changes without civil war, this new moralizing will require a tremendous increase in the use of public authority to alter the way in which established organizations and governments operate. There is a serious question as to whether American governments and the American people are fully prepared for this. The response may be to declare disorder unlawful. But in a country with a habit of freedom repression tends to produce the opposite effect.

Politics in an Age of Disorder:
The Eclipse of Political Man

Every age will thus produce its own politics. And clearly the politics of moralizing will be very different from the politics of quiescence. Yet in the confusion of change, the changes themselves are extremely difficult to identify with any precision. We can speak in generalities about grievances and moralizing, but it is difficult to be more concrete about the changes. One factor and one factor alone may, however, increase precise description of the difference between the two types of politics. This factor is political man, that very special political personality elevated during the age of political quiescence. The ups and downs of political man provide something of a tracer element to the politics of his own times and possibly an opening glance into the politics of the present and the future.

Political man has been around ever since there was a politics, and we could hardly live without him. But during political quiescence political man is not only on tap; he is on top. And when a nation is politically quiescent for the better part of three decades, the impression begins to spread that political man is a moral necessity, not merely a useful functionary. Alternatives to political man come to represent chaos. Political man, democracy, and peace come, by definition, to be inseparably joined. S. M. Lipset, in the dedication of *Political Man,* expressed the hope that his children would "grow up in a more democratic and, therefore, more peaceful world." Political quiescence produces the impression that the only alternative to peace is war; the only alternative to political man must be violent man.

The politics of quiescence elevates political man because he is a man of ultimate flexibility. He possesses the skills of the best negotiator, the patience of Job, the values of a huckster, and the kind heart of an aging prostitute. He is a man who searches until he finds a basis of agreement, and there is always a basis of agreement because, it is assumed, politics cannot handle big disagreements. Whether we are talking about a political broker who prefers vague legislation to clear legislation or a university broker who would give the university away to avoid defining what he shall defend we are talking about a man who has no program, no ideology, and makes it a point not to have one. He can make a virtue of having no goals because during his period of dominance there is no big problem of goals. Institutions and organizations are working rather well. Negotiating talents are precisely useful because life will go on pretty much as it is whether the negotiations go well or not. Political man, therefore, does not create peace. He assumes the existence of peace. His methods work because peace has already been established. When there is no peace, he is rarely the man who can achieve it.

Political man is a hypercivilized man, a political dandy. The effect of hypercivilization on politics can perhaps be best understood by comparing it to what civilized society tends to do to love. In civilized society, seduction must be preferred to rape. Sex brings people together, but if sexual violence is to be kept within strict limits, seduction must be established as the most acceptable sexual relationship. (At first this sounds quite uncomplicated.) But eventually, seduction comes to be seen as a positive virtue rather than a mere necessity for social peace. We come to admire those who are good at seduction, and some people become particularly adept at it. And as the manipulative aspects of sex are elevated higher and higher, love comes to be seen as a kind of rape, for love is, after all, a form of involuntary possession. Introduction of love to sex produces emotion, instability, pain, even hatred. Love idealizes its object; idealization involves the imposition of an entire model of behavior; and no person ever fully lived up to an ideal that love imposed on him (or her). *Playboy* represents the civilized ethic in the extreme. But so do all the sexology books that give advice on manipulation without actually knowing the identities of any of the couples and their particular relationships. American society may never eliminate love from sex as effectively as some bourgeois and aristocratic societies have done through the institutional arranged marriage. But its purpose is the same.

In politics, the civilized society also tends to prefer the arts of seduction to those of love. Men are elevated to high positions precisely because they are skilled in the arts of politics *qua* seduction. This is called "bargaining," and "negotiation," and "compromise"; in some circles it is called "the art of politics."

Political man is also associated with the "end of ideology," because ideology is love in the political sphere. Ideology is the embrace of a whole future state of affairs. Ideology is moralizing on a grand scale. And whenever ideology is expanding, the need for political man will be contracting.

The political man of the past epoch of political quiescence is neither a liberal nor a conservative—nor anything else. He worships at the shrine of process, and he counts his treasures in large numbers of small units. The operation can be a success whether the patient lives or dies. If we were all political men and the Eichmann trial had been in the United States, Eichmann's most effective defense would have been that he had not formulated extermination policy, that he took the job to keep a *real* Nazi from getting it, and that thanks to his efforts the body count was merely 6 million rather than 8 million or more. If all of us were political men, we would have treated Hitler as evil not because his ideology was evil but because he was an ideologist who did not believe in compromising.

No society could run for very long unless powerful people agreed to reason together—indeed, to compromise at the mere margins of life. But, we are beginning to discover, neither do societies operate very well when this process of compromising is thought to be sufficient as well as necessary. Political man deliberately gives politics and government a narrow perspective. However broad his mind, however bold his temperament, political man is not political man unless he conducts himself according to the immediate situation and the small departures that can be made from it without disrupting or deranging the positions of all the participants. Political man has a narrow perspective because he believes narrowness is the right way.

Approval of his conduct is of course based on the assumption, almost never articulated, that our society is so fragile that any serious departure from political seduction would mean chaos. Societies are better off doing tomorrow exactly what they are doing today with a little bit of change around the edges. In effect, therefore, political seduction justifies itself in the apocalyptic myth of the fragile society and grounds itself in a profound, even if unintended, conservatism.

Political man is basically the political version of organization man. If he is a brilliant thinker, that only makes him a better technician. This makes for a terrific adjustment, because all technicians—bureaucrats and politicians—have their techniques in common. This is the essence of political quiescence, for it means, among other things, that a political system run by political man will minimize conflict. Military technicians, for example, work well with political technicians because they too have no long-range goals. This may even eliminate conflict. But what happens to a system based, supposedly, on conflict? We are saved the perils of military men in politics, but we are deprived of meaningful counterpoise between civilian and military points of view. This more than anything else explains the slow but unstoppable escalation in Vietnam beginning in 1963. Perhaps this is why there were so few resignations in opposition to the war during that period and yet so many officials, once out of office, who claim sincerely to have opposed the escalation. An incremental approach, whether to escalation or to desegregation, gives very little cause for formulation of clear political oppositions. Opposition is literally demoralized. And the biggest trouble with political man is that he would probably agree with this analysis and proclaim it as his justification rather than his damnation. Political man gives us the peace of quiescence. What if occasionally we want something more dynamic?

During the past era of quiescence, politics was replaced by sports as America's top mass entertainment, and this development may help clarify the distinction between the politics of quiescence and the politics to come. Sports may be the only remaining mass phenomenon with a strong ethical basis. In any sports event, there is an a priori standard against which to measure behavior. There are clear issues and conflicts among well-defined adversaries. There is also a clear definition of defeat and victory. To bring the comparison closer to home, the biggest enemy of sports is gambling. This is not merely because some gamblers may destroy the ethics of the situation by rigging a few games and instilling doubt in all the other games. Gambling is the enemy of sports when it introduces ambiguity into the issues between adversaries. The amateur and innocent spectator will always have the excitement of a clear issue. But a sport is ruined for the man who looks at it through the gambler's odds and point spreads. (For example, the gamblers can arrange such a point spread that Notre Dame could not beat Vassar in football.) The gambler reduces victory and defeat to manageable increments. Political man attempts to do the same thing in politics, by reducing clear-cut issues into manageable increments. Sports and politics begin with an ethical basis. The middleman in either profession may perform a useful function by helping to define and redefine the struggle. But as the experience, whether politics or sports, becomes more indirect, through the greater intervention of the wiles and definitions of the middleman, the ethical basis becomes more remote, and the outcome less plausible. We may soon enter an era of quiescence in sports too.

All this focuses on the epoch we seem to be passing out of. As we move into a new political age and quiescence is supplanted, political man will enter into an eclipse—until political quiescence returns. Political man will find the new techniques alien to him and the new demands and movements a threat to him and his society. Political man will be overshadowed and demoted by persons who are searching for new groups rather than attempting to form new coalitions among old groups. Even the outer fringe, the fanatics of left and right, will help provide the standards by which new groups will be organized and will also help shape the new political techniques, though none of the fanatical fringe may ever be particularly powerful. Race will shape the new leadership and the new techniques, because it is the one issue that cuts across and intertwines with all the issues in our time.

All this means that the new politics will be manned by persons who can deal comfortably with whole peoples and whole communities, with whole models of man rather than with specialized roles and particularistic features of persons. The new political personalities will know how to formalize new realities rather than merely to manipulate old formalities. There are risks in this. If the level of emotion gets too high, strange bedfellows will not lie down together. But there are gains, and these outweigh the risks, because anarchy is not the alternative to political man and his kind of technique.

Juridical Democracy and the Politics of Disorder

When I was writing *The End of Liberalism* some four years ago,[1] I was primarily concerned with effectively attacking political quiescence by analyzing the self-defeating character of its pluralist ideological base and its conservative and counterproductive policies. To my surprise, the book was regarded as too negative even by many who admired the analysis. It had not occurred to me, until well after publication, that the positive alternatives to interest-group liberalism would not be clearly implied in the critique.

"Juridical democracy" was the term I coined for the most desirable positive alternative to interest-group democracy. Basically, juridical democracy is a name for formal democracy, a majority rule democracy limited only by the absolute requirement that government be run as closely as possible according to the way it says

[1] Theodore J. Lowi, *The End of Liberalism: Ideology, Policy and the Crisis of Public Authority* (New York: W. W. Norton & Co., Inc. 1969).

it is run. The most outstanding feature of juridical democracy, I felt then and feel now, is rule-of-law, which contrasts in the extreme from the pluralist practice of policy-without-law. Running the country through broad grants of authority to administrators is no less irresponsible and undemocratic than running a country through broad grants of authority by the king to his representatives or through divine grants of authority to the king himself. In a juridical democracy, chaos is preferable to a bad program. One of the primary purposes of this book is to show that chaos is not so bad as it is painted.

Some other readers of *The End of Liberalism* found the positive side of the critique, but it hit them as unrealistic. I was, to them, guilty of an unpardonable sin. I had not committed a social science. Far worse, I had committed a civics. It is plainly unsophisticated to argue that formalisms are more than humbug. As one critic put it, juridical democracy bears no relation "to any known actualities of modern political government." This observation makes entirely clear what I had failed to anticipate in *The End of Liberalism* and must seek to account for in this volume: I had not anticipated the fact that those nurtured on pluralism as an ideology, those whose entire political lives had been enveloped in the governmental principles of delegation and manipulation ("political government"), would find formal democracy totally unreal, alien, and even offensive.

Therefore, this book intends to show more explicitly that there are alternatives to political government (that is, pluralistic government, policy without law, or whatever one wants to call it) and that the alternatives are just as realistic as the existing modus operandi. Granted, pure and unrestrained group process does have a natural and predictable set of outcomes. This is why the study of government by pluralists seems to be realistic and sophisticated. I have taken on the task of showing that there are other social processes that lead to alternative outcomes. These outcomes, particularly formalistic democracy and rule of law, are just as natural and actual as the actualities of modern political government.

The basis of pluralism and political quiescence is the organized group and group interactions, with political man holding the whole together through delegation and negotiation. The basis of the alternative process and the alternative principle of government, I intend to show, is civil liberties, the individual, and the mass, held together by a structure of formal government and law rather than by political man and his reputation for leadership.

Chapters 1 and 2 seek primarily to locate the social process that ends in formalism. Chapter 1 is a sociological study of the formation of the major groups in American society and how the pattern of their rise and rigidification makes it impossible for pluralists to continue to assume that an unregulated group process will give us an acceptable political government. There is an iron law of decadence, or a rule of rigidification, that must somehow be taken into account and is not taken into account by students of political quiescence.

Chapter 2 identifies a political process, just as profound and realistic as the pluralistic process, that culminates in an approximation of juridical democracy. That is to say, *juridical democracy is grounded in real social processes.* By demonstrating this I hope to overcome the most serious weakness in its appeal to those liberals who are desperately searching for explanations and alternatives for their present plight. I could perhaps confuse my audience and confound my critics by proving that formalism is grounded in Kant and constitutionalism, but for the modern mind it is more effective to show that formulations are realistic rather than merely scholastic.

Chapters 3, 4, and 5 are efforts to look at movements and other disorders in the context of actual governmental structures. In that context, we are really talking about civil liberties and the impact that governmental responses to disorder will have on the individual and his exercise of civil liberties. If the first two chapters culminate in the argument that movements and other such disorders will end in some pretty good rules of law, Part II suggests an additional advantage to a system based on an appreciation of the uses of disorder—free mass opinion and mass movements operate primarily as resources for the legislative branch. Efforts to repress the exercise of civil liberties on the grounds that it is disorder or efforts to coopt it on the grounds that cooption is the only form of peace work basically to the advantage of bureaucracies and the least democratic aspects of government. (Such efforts to coopt or repress also work to the advantage of the most privileged elements of society.) This is why I call Part II "Freedom *from* Association: Civil Liberties and the Failure of Governments."

Part III is concerned with the question of where the best and most useful disorder comes from. Inasmuch as enlightened disorder is better than unenlightened disorder and higher education has come to be our biggest industry, the universities deserve a careful assessment as major political forces. Calling this part "Higher Education: The Roots of Constructive Alienation" is obviously more an expression of hope than a statement of fact. But throughout the two chapters I am trying to establish above all else that the same issues and the same principles are at work here as in the governmental sphere. This means that efforts to deal with disorder that are governed largely by the techniques of political man may very well be counterproductive. We could easily find ourselves, as a consequence, with universities completely indistinguishable from other service stations. When that happens we will have come closer to a totalitarian society, because a totalitarian society is one in which all institutions come to resemble one another and in which there are no systematic and institutionalized sources of alienation.

Chapter 8 returns more explicitly to the original concerns. It is simply another part of a long and continuing effort to assess law as a political force and to establish law as a principle of democratic government far more capable than any other principle for dealing with disorder without managing it, coopting it, or suppressing it.

TJL

Spring, 1971

Contents

PART IV
LAW AND THE USES OF DISORDER

PART I

FREEDOM OF ASSOCIATION: GROUPS, MOVEMENTS, AND SOCIETY'S CAPACITY FOR CHANGE

1

Group Politics and the Iron Law of Decadence

A strange thing happened during the summer of 1969. In several major cities workers were picketing unions. To be exact, blacks were picketing the building trades unions. Union members pictured themselves defending their hard-earned right to control and protect skilled work. The picketers pictured themselves as paying most of the costs of the rights the unions were defending.

Not very long ago American trade unionists might have laughed indignantly at Shaw's epigram on trade unionism. But by 1969 many trade unions, and in particular the building trade unions, had indeed become "the capitalism of the proletariat." Worse yet, they appeared to be the embodiment of perhaps the worst kind of narrow-minded capitalism. Black demands for collective recognition were being met in 1969 by hard-line tactics, including strike-breaking through use of local police forces.

In Philadelphia a quota system was ultimately forced on the unions. This solution seemed likely to spread to other cities; still other solutions might be found elsewhere. But even if some kind of Philadelphia plan ultimately succeeds throughout the building trades, the underlying problem will be repeated many times in many unions. At some future point we will find ourselves writing the same kind of story all over again, because even the fully integrated building trades unions will have to defend some other status quo against some other movement. The next issue may be conveyor belt housing and the problem of technological unemployment. Or it may be some newly arrived ethnic or racial group. But the story will be about the same.

The story is about the same in other sectors. It is not limited to narrow-minded union leaders, though it is hard to imagine anyone more narrow-minded than old-line union leaders. The same pattern will be found among agricultural and business groups, indeed, among groups of every class and race. The pattern is not even affected by the economic context. A dynamic and competitive market is perhaps even more likely to produce conservative groups than markets dominated by monopolies. As Daniel Bell reports,

in the highly competitive or small-unit-sized fields, the unions have stepped in and provided a monopoly structure to the markets, limiting the entry of firms into the industry, establishing price lines, etc. This has been true most notably in the coal industry, in the garment industry, and in the construction trades.[1]

The same pattern prevails among the business groups. Trade associations become even more necessary in decentralized markets: When the number of firms is greater, the threat of competition is stronger. Three of the most famous trade associations—the National Association of Real Estate Boards, the National Association of Retail Druggists, and the American Medical Association—administer to highly decentralized markets.[2]

Industrial societies are almost inevitably group societies. The division of labor, the specialization of functions, and a host of other social complexities provide an infinity of bases for organization. The rigid class structures of preindustrial and early industrial societies do not give way to classless societies. The numerous class does not devour the less numerous. Rather, both disappear, or are overshadowed, by the multiplication of strata. The proletariat breaks up into several layers which are in turn cut across

---

[1] Daniel Bell, *The End of Ideology* (New York: The Free Press, 1960), p. 210.

[2] See Chapter 3.

by basic differences in the plight and interests of workers in different industries and sectors. Bourgeois classes are even more susceptible to subdivision.

This is all very well, especially because it seems to happen whether there is a proletarian revolution or not. But a group or pluralist society is only one particular adjustment to a particular phase of economic development. It is not a millennial solution, any more than a classless society would be. Whatever social contrivances man devises, he pays a price for every gain. For the average man the pluralist society is a clear gain over a highly class-stratified society. But there are costs and the costs may be cumulative. After decades of appreciating the benefits of social pluralism, it is time we began to calculate the costs. And just as we located our gains in the many groups that emerge to represent the many strata in pluralist societies, so we are likely to find most of our costs there.

Groups provide a great deal of necessary social efficiency. They are effective means of articulating and representing interests and providing low-level social controls that reduce the need for governmental coercion. But the very success of established groups is a mortgage against a future of new needs that are not yet organized or are not readily accommodated by established groups. One of modern society's great challenges is how to reap the benefits of groups and at the same time to minimize the costs. Among the costs the greatest is the "iron law of decadence," that tendency of all organizations to maintain themselves at the expense of needed change and innovation.

Groups show remarkable similarities in their modes of construction and in their ultimate impact on society and the political system. Examination of the most important groups—the organized sectors of the economy—suggests that the similarities are not only quite close and profound but also seem to involve unavoidable patterns of development. Here, as the next two chapters attempt to show, is the basis of the most serious dilemma facing industrial society: how to be efficient and stable without being rigid in structure and reactionary in results.

Agriculture: The Classic Case

After the Civil War economic and social conditions in the United States were ripe for radical change, especially in the agricultural sector. From the very earliest times agriculture had been outside the mainstream of economic development in America. Agriculture remained decentralized and dispersed in the face of industrial concentration. It remained local while the rest of the economy became regional and national. After the Civil War all these factors came into focus as agriculture entered the money economy, through a transportation system not of its own making, in a market very much under the control of nonagricultural interests.

The commercialization of agriculture into regional and national markets made the otherwise isolated and independent farmer aware not only of his neighbors but of all those who shared his status. All farmers suddenly found themselves subject to transportation, storage, exchange, and bank problems. Not only did they discover themselves to be something of a poor cousin in the American economic family, but they found out what it was like to be on the receiving and not on the delivering end of a production chain. The situation was aggravated by a particular kind of instability that was perhaps worse than simply being depressed. Such was the relation of agriculture to the capitalist system that its prices rose higher than other sectors during booms and fell lower than the others during deflationary periods. No pattern was better designed to excite a social movement.[3]

Farmer reactions to this new turn of economic events were predictably intense, though piecemeal and somewhat slow to pick up velocity. That is to say, for a long time obvious and intense

[3] For a good brief treatment of the economics of agriculture, see Walter Adams, ed., *The Structure of American Industry* (New York: Macmillan, 1961), chap. 1; see also Murray R. Benedict, *Farm Policies of the United States 1790–1950* (New York: Twentieth Century Fund, 1953).

common irritants were not enough to bring about a national movement. But when the movement did begin to gather momentum, it is significant that it took the form of a fraternal organization. The Grange movement, officially the National Grange Order of the Patrons of Husbandry, was founded in 1867 as a direct expression of agrarian discontent. At first based primarily in the upper Mississippi Valley, it spread with each turn of economic adversity until, by 1874, it had reached its peak membership of about 750,000.

The Grange never became a truly national organization, though it was extremely strong throughout the entire central region of the United States and was a measurable force elsewhere. However, it established the pattern of agricultural organization and group representation throughout the remainder of the nineteenth century. It was fraternal, it was highly excitable and intense, and it identified as a unit all agrarian persons and interests. In this it was something of an exclusive organization, especially in comparison with the agricultural societies that had developed before the American Revolution and had existed throughout the first half of the nineteenth century. A particularly important distinction lay in the political militance of the Grange. It sought and got some of the most important regulatory legislation in the history of the American states, and it was responsible for garnering a rather large array of services from many states and from the Federal government. In fact, most early expansions of Federal activities were in response to agricultural demands. Though the farmers failed for many years to get Federal regulation of railroads or other businesses that affect agriculture, there was greater and more immediate success in other areas, such as coinage of silver, agricultural credit, expansion of land give-aways, a great expansion of research and other agricultural services, and improvements in statistical and marketing aids.

But the Grange never really succeeded as a national social movement. According to Handlin, disillusionment set in during the 1880s and the organization retreated to its state and local Grange strongholds. These local organizations withdrew from both business and politics, confining themselves almost exclusively to social and fraternal functions.[4]

The political aspects of the agricultural movement did not disappear with the decline of the Grange; they were simply taken over by another, more militant and politicized organization, the Farmers Alliance. The Alliance was truly the vanguard of the agrarian movement, because it led the farmers into a new political status. It provided the leadership and the continuity to turn the agrarian movement into a political movement with its own political party. Thus, the movement turned to another organizational phase.

The Alliance, and the various components that it had taken over on the way to national dominance, turned agricultural grievances into a program. According to Handlin, this programmatic material was intermixed with the already well-established "tradition of religious revivalism."[5] By the end of the 1880s the agricultural movement, though more complex than implied here, was imbued with political fervor, political purpose, strong leadership, and solid doctrine. Its greatest stroke came in 1892 with the formation of the People's Party.

According to McConnell, the People's Party "seemed to threaten the destruction of all the economic winnings of a capitalism so far victorious."[6] Though lacking in detail, McConnell's account probably best captures the spirit of that period. Though the scope of the disturbance was narrower than it seemed,[7] this agrarian movement and its party was the most influential force of that era. Such men as James B. Weaver (the Populist presidential candidate in 1892), William Jennings Bryan, and "Sockless Jerry" Simpson were absorbed into the Democratic Party, but so was the greatest part of their program and, in the American tradition, their reason for being.

[4] Oscar Handlin, *The History of the United States,* vol. 2 (New York: Holt, Rinehart and Winston, 1968), p. 93.

[5] *Ibid.,* pp. 162–163.

[6] Grant McConnell, *The Decline of Agrarian Democracy* (Berkeley: University of California Press, 1953), p. 3.

[7] *Ibid.*

Disappearance of the national party by the turn of the century did not signal the end of the agrarian movement, but only its turn into a third, strictly business-minded organizational, phase. When the movement unfolded it had been seen as a "religious revival, a crusade, a pentecost of politics in which a tongue of flame sat upon every man, and each spake as the spirit gave him utterance."[8] But soon after the turn of the century, agrarianism began to express itself in a completely different form: "The monumental fact of the period is the rise of a structure of political power based on farm organization representing a repudiation of the traditional agrarian distrust of power. . . ."[9] Granted, not all the old spirit had disappeared, and some never would.[10] However, it would be in a minor key, and the dominant style would be rational organization along business lines for purposes of making realistic government policy—and for the ultimate purpose of controlling the market insofar as it affects agriculture. Again at the risk of over-simplification, the reality of the new agriculture in this era was the commodity organization. This was a national pattern though no one commodity organization reached national proportions. The only national organization of any great importance was the American Farm Bureau Federation, founded in 1919, which came along well after commodity organizations were formed but which represents the same principle of organization.[11]

Each commodity organization is rather tightly conceived around its own needs and the region within which it is primarily produced.

[8] Elizabeth N. Barr, quoted in McConnell, *Decline of Agrarian Democracy*, p. 4.

[9] *Ibid.*, p. 1.

[10] For a good coverage of the efforts to maintain the old spirit and the problems of trying to do so, see *ibid.*, chap. 4.

[11] For accounts of the commodity basis of agricultural organization, see Murray R. Benedict, *Farm Policies of the United States, 1790–1950;* Theodore J. Lowi, *The End of Liberalism* (New York: Norton, 1969), chap. 4; and Wesley McCune, *The Farm Bloc* (Garden City: Doubleday, 1943). For accounts of the Farm Bureau Federation, see McConnell, *Decline of Agrarian Democracy,* and Orville M. Kile, *The Farm Bureau Through Three Decades* (Baltimore: Waverly Press, 1948).

Though there is obviously some overlap of membership, these farm organizations, according to Key, "seldom unite for legislative purposes."[12] They sometimes did get together in a farm bloc during the 1920s, they can collaborate within or without the Farm Bureau Federation, and they can on occasion—for example, during the 1930s with the New Deal—unite within the framework of a political party. But they are separate and distinct units of formal organization. The American Farm Bureau Federation is famous for its rational, near bureaucratic mode of organization. Zeigler, in fact, refers to the Federation as the "triumph of formal organization."[13]

Elements of the old agrarian spirit occasionally reemerge. Occasionally a charismatic or emotional leader will arise, as George Peek did during an important time of trouble in the 1920s. But the prevailing pattern of agricultural organization in the seventy years since the height of the movement has been the establishment of stable alliances among its own parts and between its parts and government agencies for the purpose of stabilizing agricultural markets. Even during the 1920s, temporary return of agrarian emotionalism, the overwhelming purpose of the farm bloc was to use government to solve agriculture's problems in precisely the same way that big business had solved its problems. Farm leaders even referred to their goal as "making the tariff work for agriculture." No longer was the goal to overturn the capitalist system, either by inflating or dismantling it. And no longer did the dominating agrarian interests have any patience with those who might try such a thing.

Zeigler provides some interesting examples of the resistance of the Farm Bureau and the commodity organizations against other forms of politicizing agriculture, especially during the 1920s and early 1930s.[14] However, the most important manifestations of

[12] V. O. Key, Jr., *Politics, Parties and Pressure Groups,* 5th ed. (New York: Crowell, 1964), p. 40.

[13] Harmon Zeigler, *Interest Groups in American Society* (Englewood Cliffs, N.J.: Prentice-Hall, 1964), p. 174 ff.

[14] Zeigler, *ibid.,* pp. 179–180.

organizational conservatism in the politics of agriculture can be found in the relations between the prevailing agricultural organizations during the past twenty years and the way each uses its relationship with some governmental agency to keep itself distinct from other groups and to stabilize its relationships with other groups. I have reported in detail elsewhere on this pattern and will only make scant reference to it here.[15] In the Federal government, there are at least ten self-governing systems of policy-making, each of which is built on an institutionalized relationship between some bureau in the Department of Agriculture, some agricultural interest group, and some protective committee or subcommittee of Congress. Each system is built up from the grass roots, and at the grass roots level each tends to be built along the same lines as the national level, with a formal policy-making committee comprised of local farmers whose primary interests are in the commodities and problems of that area.

Despite the fact that the farm population has declined and that agriculture no longer holds the extremely high place it once did in the American belief system, every effort to reorganize the department during the last twenty years has failed. Even minor efforts to reduce the number of local, self-governing committees have failed. Efforts to fuse the price support local committees with the conservation local committees, despite their obvious interdependence, have been vetoed either by the commodity interests that control the parity process or by the Farm Bureau and other interests that control aspects of the conservation process. This has been repeated time after time in other areas.[16]

Agriculture was earlier than labor or commerce in organizing on a national scale for pressure-group activity. Agriculture was also early in the invention of means of stabilizing and perpetuating whatever organization pattern they had managed to achieve. Agriculture was, finally, very early in discovering that the best way to perpetuate an organization is to capture a government agency and

---

[15] Lowi, *End of Liberalism*, p. 102 ff.
[16] See also Charles Hardin, *The Politics of Agriculture* (Glencoe: The Free Press, 1952).

to use governmental power to maintain established patterns inside the group and between a given group and all other competing groups.

And this brings us back to a major theme of this book: Group needs for stability seem to be so great that they have helped to convert modern governments into additional means of system maintenance for groups rather than for the society at large. Government sponsorship and maintenance of organized groups has become a very important aspect of contemporary democratic ideology.[17]

The House of Labor:
Revolutionary Goals, Defensive Organization

Well before the onset of the Civil War, trade unionism had ceased to be considered a conspiracy, even in the laissez-faire United States. The most important case concerning the question of whether a union is per se illegal, *Commonwealth* v. *Hunt*,[18] had been handed down in 1842. This case was influential throughout the northeast industrial areas, and though there were few cases in other states to compare to it, it is generally thought that the doctrine of criminal conspiracy went into disuse rather quickly after the Massachusetts case. The use of injunctions against strikes continued well into the twentieth century, but this was based not on the doctrine that strikes were illegal per se, but that they must be judged in terms of the ends sought.[19]

[17] See Lowi, *The End of Liberalism,* where it is argued that pluralist democracy develops an ideology, "interest-group liberalism," which is based on the faith that if government will maintain groups, groups will in turn provide general social stability.

[18] 45 Mass. 111 (1842).

[19] See John H. Leek, *Government and Labor in the U. S.* (New York: Rinehart, 1952), p. 20 ff. See also C. O. Gregory, *Labor and the Law* (New York: Norton, 1946).

Nevertheless, trade unionism emerged rather fitfully and almost as though it had been a clandestine movement. That is to say, much like agriculture, modern trade unionism began in a series of fraternal and relatively militant efforts. During the many years before the American business system finally adjusted to the revolution in labor relationships, developments in union organization had moved in fits and starts. But virtually all the early efforts were of a fraternal character, especially those efforts that moved beyond local craft guilds and attempted to combine trade organizations across a large city or among units in more than one city. Very often the term "brotherhood" was in the title of the parent organization.

Leek and others report on the character of efforts to link up labor groups in what today would be considered a city central trades council, or an international.[20] However, the best case in point for this early period is the history of the International Typographical Union (ITU). It had roots extending back to the revolution, it had thirty-four major locals by 1860, and it was composed of the intellectuals, perhaps even the aristocracy, of labor. Yet, despite this exceptional basis for rationality, the ITU was formed with strong elements of fraternal bonding. Their formal organization was highly decentralized. Lipset reports that the national headquarters had very little to do and that the first full-time officers were not instituted until twenty-five years after the founding. He also reports that these locals were strongly bound together inside the ITU by secret societies.[21] The first mention of secret societies among the printers is in 1843. The early societies were mainly attempts to protect a single local against the pressures of a single employer; but in time they developed from the secret infrastructure of the movement into the nonsecret ITU. The first effort in this direction was called the Order of Faust, a movement to organize the leaders in New York City, Albany, Washington,

---

[20] Leek, *Government and Labor in the U. S.*, p. 22 ff. See also Handlin, *History of the United States*, p. 100 ff., and Bell, *End of Ideology*, p. 213 ff.
[21] S. M. Lipset, James Coleman, and Martin Trow, *Union Democracy* (Garden City: Doubleday, 1962), pp. 18 ff. and 37 ff.

Cincinnati, Boston, and Philadelphia. A more substantial version was formed in 1857, very shortly after the official formation of the ITU. After that, there was no long period without a brotherhood underlying the ITU.[22]

Some early union movements were not, strictly speaking, craft movements. The Molly Maguires, an organization with a brief but rather spectacular history during the 1870s, was composed largely of coal miners and other unskilled workers, mainly Irish. The Molly Maguires were apparently a militant, terrorist labor organization formed within an already extant fraternal society, the Ancient Order of Hibernians. During the same period there was the first effort, in a less fraternal movement, to unite all labor in a single organization, the National Labor Union (NLU). Its life was even briefer than that of the Molly Maguires. Moreover, it was the Molly Maguires rather than the National Labor Union who dramatized the plight of labor and led to the later and more successful efforts to unite all labor.

The first real success in breaking down the fears of individual laborers and the reluctance of preexisting craft unions was the Knights of Labor,[23] which had emerged at the same time as the NLU, but which lasted longer and had far greater effects. It was also for most of its life a secret, fraternal organization and remained secret into the 1880s despite a very large membership. Though it left few famous names in the pages of American history, it was nonetheless militant and committed to the organization of labor as a class.[24]

The Knights had political as well as narrow labor interests, and were involved in a number of important struggles, some of a re-

---

[22] *Ibid.,* pp. 38–43.

[23] The full title was the Noble Order of the Knights of Labor, founded in 1869 by Uriah Stephens, a Philadelphia tailor.

[24] The best known leader of the Knights was Terrence V. Powderly, who became Grand Master Workman in 1879. Apparently he enunciated most of the general views of the organization, and these were oriented toward including anyone who toiled, wage or salaried, unskilled or skilled, black or white, and so on. Appropriately, perhaps, he is memorialized by Powderly, Alabama, a dingy industrial suburban village near the Birmingham steel complexes.

formist nature and others more revolutionary. Perhaps because of the continued hostility of American business and government to militancy in trade unions, the Knights remained militant to the end —an end that was accelerated by a few cases of violence, not the least of which was the Haymarket Riot of 1886. Olson argues convincingly that all effective unionism will be violent unless it is supported by government policy that makes collective bargaining legal and the crossing of picket lines illegal.[25]

The Knights, like the Molly Maguires, tended mainly to drama- tize the plight of the worker and the weaknesses of the system. In this manner the two organizations had brought labor as a move- ment into a period of labor consciousness never before experi- enced; but neither type of organization could go further. As Greenstone puts it, "the Knights failed because they never seriously faced, let alone solved, the problem of organizing the divided and self-interested American working class. There was a fatal dis- junction between the order's ambitious goal of uniting all workers in a single organization and the vagueness with which it defined its specific constituency and its strategy and tactics."[26] Thus, what we have left is the sense of a movement without an organizational vanguard or core. Labor had gone through a phase and would go no further without a basic break with the existing organization level and leadership. This is precisely what happened with the emergence of the American Federation of Labor (AFL).

The AFL, formed in 1881 as the Federation of Organized Trade and Labor Unions, was from the beginning a more ration- ality-oriented organization. Greenstone reports on such distinctive devices as the refusal to include nonworkers or to mix members of different crafts in the same local, high dues, and high benefits and services to individual members.[27]

The unquestioned leader throughout the first forty years of AFL

[25] On the relation of unionism to violence, see Mancur Olson, *The Logic of Collective Action* (New York: Schocken Books, 1968), chap. 3 and the citations therein.
[26] J. David Greenstone, *Labor in American Politics* (New York: Knopf, 1969), p. 21.
[27] *Ibid.*, p. 23.

history was Samuel Gompers. Though Gompers apparently possessed a considerable amount of charisma, he was basically a theoretician and an organizer. His notion of business unionism was a brilliant encapsulation of the needs of American labor and its problematic relationships with the outside world. Gompers focused, articulated, and directed the goals of labor and, moreover, related the plight of the individual wage earner to his role as a member of organized labor. This latter seems to be an essential connection that an organizational theorist must make if organizing elements are to take hold. In any case, Gompers proceeded to differentiate his organization from other organizations competing for control of the labor movement. He declared war on the Knights of Labor and their practice of allowing dissidents from other unions to join their ranks.[28] He also took measures to establish the supremacy of national organizations over locals, in sharp contrast to the ITU and other nationals and internationals.

As the labor movement nationalized and its fraternal origins receded into the background, the American Federation of Labor came to dominate all other national contenders. Gompers, in fact, had provided one solution for both organizational and doctrinal problems; in so doing he had brought a large part of the labor movement into a new phase. The AFL did not come to represent the entire labor movement by any means. Nevertheless, it is typical of what was happening in most of that part of the labor movement that it did not directly influence or represent.

Another example of this move into a second phase will be found in the railroad brotherhoods. Well before the turn of the century these brotherhoods had added such rational incentives as insurance to their fraternal ties. This is a particularly significant incentive in an industry where injury was frequent and insurance protection difficult to buy. Every advance in insurance service signified the replacement of fraternal with contractual relationships. Olson and Toner report that the conductors' union ultimately

[28] See, for example, Handlin, *History of the United States,* p. 105: "Such dual unionism, which permitted employers to play one labor organization against another, was a threat to all artisans."

went so far as to emphasize its insurance program "to the virtual exclusion of all else."[29] Even more widespread than insurance as a mechanism for converting unions into contractual organizations was seniority. Even where unions did not possess a monopoly or closed shop they could maintain a highly rational and efficient member relationship wherever they could formalize employment through seniority. In later years, of course, other contractual aspects were added to union membership. Perhaps the most significant of these is job classification, in which rights and obligations of work are described as meticulously as machines are designed by engineers.

All this is part of an institutionalization and formalization that has never really ceased since the turn of the century. True, there are currents and countercurrents to indicate that the old spirit is not entirely dead, but these fragments are only occasionally expressed with enough force to remind a large public that they are not yet entirely gone. Labor history is occasionally marked by the emergence of such militant and narrowly defined submovements as the socialists, the Wobblies, and so on. More importantly, the last seventy-five years have also witnessed the emergence of industrial unionism, which is a very large part of the labor movement and not merely a fragmentary offshoot. But industrial unionism is simply a delayed catching up of one whole segment of labor, and it seems fairly clear that industrial unionism has gone through phases similar to those of craft unionism. The rise of the Congress of Industrial Organizations (CIO) and associated industrial unions, such as United Auto, Aircraft and Agricultural Implements Workers (UAW), is an interesting study in movement for its own sake, and all the more interesting as an offshoot of the AFL. The AFL during the 1930s was simply unable to incorporate the new spirit of industrial unionism, which had begun as a committee within the AFL itself. Twenty years afterward, the CIO and AFL were able to merge. But this was a highly superficial and highly contractual merger of two quite distinctive organizations willing

[29] Jerome Toner, in Olson, *Logic of Collective Action*, p. 72.

to share a parent bureaucracy for certain additional contractual and rational purposes.[30] There is nothing about the labor movement since World War II that suggests any lasting departure from a highly bureaucratized organizational pattern.

However, the bureaucratization of the American labor movement does not seem to involve either a betrayal or a displacement of goals; nor can it be attributed to the latent bias of members in favor of oligarchy and bureaucracy.[31] Clearly, the original goal of the movement—union control of the labor market—remains. The rhetoric has certainly changed. But the rhetoric is really a rationalization, or operationalization, of the revolution of class relations between labor and management. Thus the goals were not lost; they were articulated and formalized.

The organizational structure produces the same pattern. Oligarchy in leadership and bureaucratization in functions, along with seniority, union shops, insurance, and job classification are "organizational imperatives."[32] And they remain so precisely because the original goals of the union have not been displaced. All the parts, ranging from the goals to the organizational principles to the individual behavior of members, have simply become articulated as part of the same functioning organization. Labor unions, perhaps more than any organizations other than formalized bureaucracies, display this extraordinarily intimate connection among goals, structures, leadership, membership and ideology.

To anticipate later analysis, it ought to be clear already why an organization involves organizational imperatives and why this means organizational conservatism. Regardless of its commitment to particular goals, the established organization will resist other organizational forms or approaches to attain these same goals. And it is precisely at this point that social pathologies arise out of successful attempts at social organization. Successful movements that become organizations do not and cannot incorporate all persons

---

[30] Walter Reuther, whose spirit and style distinguished him from other AFL-CIO leaders, eventually pulled the UAW out of the giant union; this is another indication of the remnant of militancy of some unions.

[31] See Chapter 2.

[32] Olson, *Logic of Collective Action*, p. 77.

who share in one way or another the interests being pursued by the organization. It has always been one of the fallacies implicit in pluralist democratic theory that an organization like a labor union can possibly represent the interests of all those who feel that labor unions are salient to their interests. But if this be the case, and some labor interests are not incorporated in unions, then inevitably other efforts to shape the movement will emerge.

For many years, to take one illustration, the UAW has been squelched in its efforts to alter the methods by which the established house of labor operates.[33] To look at the same problem the other way around, the building trades unions are specifically organized to prevent alternate ways of approaching construction and alternate modes of recruiting and training skilled persons. The character and drama of the problem are well illustrated by the recent series of strikes by black job seekers against the union "management." But, as *Fortune* put it, the craft unions do not simply discriminate against Negroes; they discriminate against everybody.[34] The same *Fortune* study was able to provide some indication of the degree of strict oligarchy by identifying the many important craft unions led by family dynasties. Several of the largest craft unions in the building trades were ruled with an iron hand for from twenty-five to forty years by one leader, whose son succeeded directly after the death or retirement of the father. Examples range from such internationals as the United Brotherhood of Carpenters and Joiners, whose father-son combination has ruled for considerably more than fifty years, to Local 3 of the International Brotherhood of Electrical Workers (New York), whose 38,000 members accepted Thomas Van Arsdale as business manager after having enjoyed the leadership of Thomas' father, Harry Van Arsdale, Jr., for thirty-five years. The father continues his long-standing leadership of New York's Central Labor Council.[35]

[33] This, too, is related to their break with the AFL-CIO, of course.

[34] "The Unchecked Power of the Building Trades," *Fortune Magazine*, LXXVII, December, 1968, p. 105.

[35] *Ibid.*, pp. 106–107.

Family dynasties and bureaucratic structures do not exhaust the organizational weapons used by union organizations to maintain their present modes of operation and base of stability. In the final analysis, much of labor success depends on regular and systematic support of unionism by governmental policies and agencies.[36]

McConnell cites 1932 as the dividing point in labor's attitude toward government. Prior to that time the stress was on voluntarism, and union policy was to prevent intervention by governments, as well as employers and other unions. After 1932 the AFL and eventually the other unions broke with that tradition and began to seek all kinds of government sponsorship and intervention, beginning with unemployment insurance and extending over a variety of services that we now regard as natural and inevitable.[37]

But there is still another weapon used with increasing frequency by unions in recent years. This is direct alliance with the Democratic Party. Collaboration with parties was, of course, always a means of involving government on the side of labor. Part of the tactics of business unionism was the cultivation of the myth that unions would support their friends and punish their enemies in the state legislatures, executive houses, and Congress. All this was, of course, for the purpose of influencing legislation and governmental action. However, the large unions have increasingly cast their lot exclusively with the Democratic Party—recently with the conservative wing, at that. In many cities unions have become the organizational core of the party itself. Under such conditions, the role of labor in politics is quite different. Though it can still seek favorable legislation in this way, it is also absorbing certain party organization techniques as part of its own means of directly controlling its internal processes. In other words, party techniques of organization, patronage, campaigns, public appeals, and so on are

[36] See, for example, Olson, *Logic of Collective Action,* p. 76 ff.; and Grant McConnell, *Private Power and American Democracy* (New York: Knopf, 1966) p. 299 ff.

[37] *Ibid.,* pp. 299–300.

means of maintaining union membership, quite separately from whatever legislation might be gained thereby.

Certain of these party techniques are rationalistic just as are the bureaucratic elements of conventionally designated unionism. However, a number of obviously fraternal, nonrational, elements are added whenever unions also become parties. First, it opens up the possibility of recruiting occasional charismatic persons without necessarily drawing them from the top leadership of the union. One can, in this way, enjoy the benefits of charisma and fraternity without necessarily disrupting union organization. Another advantage is the enhanced capacity to control environments without necessarily expanding union membership. A third obvious advantage is that the union can incorporate this very important, fraternal aspect of the life experiences of its members. In other words, the union—just like recreation centers, schools, insurance companies, and housing projects—is one step closer to the total incorporation of the personalities of the members. I hesitate to apply the word "totalitarian" to the unions, because it implies violence and intimidation; I mean a move toward the total by degrees, in the sense that important aspects of one's life, separate from work and work place, are being included in the concept of the union. All these comprise aspects of membership and organizational maintenance in periods of maturity.[38]

Movement to Organization in Business

One rarely thinks of social movements in modern business. Except for shopkeeper revolts, such as Poujadism in France, this sort of phenomenon is associated with the disestablished, and business,

[38] For the best treatment of this aspect of unionism, see Greenstone, *Labor in American Politics.* For good treatments of other aspects of mature trade unionism, see Bell, *End of Ideology,* chap. 11, and S. M. Lipset, *Political Man* (New York: Doubleday, 1960) chap. 12.

especially corporate business, has been very much established for well over a century. Movements are thought of as reactions to an overstabilized, overestablished, exploitative business system. However, business is not and never was in a state of equilibrium. Quite a different pattern has been prevalent for most of its history.

It was business's reaction to its own disequilibrium that led to governmental policies such as those administered by the Federal Trade Commission (FTC). The FTC, beginning in 1914, was in fact explicitly charged with curbing the disequilibrating aspects of competition. Those things defined as "unfair competition" in the Federal Trade Commission Act, the Clayton Act, and in more recent acts, such as the Robinson-Patman Act of 1938, are actually the devices inevitably used by dynamic, risk-taking entrepreneurs to expand their share of the market. Dynamic entrepreneurs were always more frightening to the complacent, and a lot more disequilibrating in real life, than anarchosyndicalists and the like. The justification for outlawing cutthroat competition was that such devices were used by people to create monopolies in an otherwise competitive sector. Ironically, it would be difficult to find a single case of monopoly or oligopoly in the United States that arose out of cutthroat competition, or unfair competition. Monopolies have arisen out of new inventions, new processes, or government policies.[39]

It is remarkable the extent to which the business system, despite its establishmentarian reputation, has shared the movement characteristics of the other sectors and the so-called lower brackets. Business dynamism has run down, but the pattern and origin of this decadence is strikingly similar to the patterns already described in the agricultural and labor sectors.

The nineteenth century was a period of fantastic growth and

[39] For a good analysis of the law and its intentions and the real meaning of unfair competition, see Alan Stone, unpublished M.A. thesis, The University of Chicago, 1969; for a classic analysis of the sources of monopoly, see Joseph Schumpeter, *Capitalism, Socialism, and Democracy* (New York: Harper, 1942), pt. 2. See also W. Adams and H. Gray, *Monopoly in America* (New York: Macmillan, 1955).

instability for the economic system of the United States. Fortunes were made and lost overnight. Slumps, booms, busts, and crazes characterized regular points in the frequently oscillating business cycle between the 1840s and World War I—the period when the United States was developing its nationalized, continental economy. There were tremendous advantages in a continental free-trade area. It was probably the single most important influence behind the rejection of the Articles of Confederation in favor of the Constitution. But the concomitant disadvantages to the individual businessman were also apparent. There were economic pressures, brought about by rising rents, interest rates, and organized labor, that were not subject to direct manipulation by business, and that wiped out profit when prices were low.

There are two basic types of reaction to these disequilibria in business, and both of them manifest strong movement characteristics (that is, dynamism followed by decadence) in business. The first reaction is, of course, control of the environment through size —through oligopoly if necessary and monopoly if possible. The second of these was business organization in essentially political forms, the most important and lasting aspect of which is the trade association.[40]

Capitalist Organization in a Single Firm

It is fascinating to trace the history of the consolidation of a large oligopolistic or monopolistic business or to discover the extent to which it goes through the basic movement characteristics. The best example of this pattern, both because it is the most direct portrayal of it and because it is the most clearly documented case, is that of General Motors. The autobiography of Alfred P. Sloan is a major contribution to American history and to sociological

[40] Other types of adjustment include pools, other market-sharing devices, trusts, holding companies, and so on. Most of these were declared illegal early in the history of modern business in the United States, but in any case they do not constitute anything special with regard to the behavioral characteristics of concern here. They are mentioned briefly below.

theory.[41] In it, he carefully traces all decisions, crises, and phases through which this gigantic organization had come from its relatively tiny infancy. Only a few of the high spots can be mentioned here, but Sloan's autobiography is strongly recommended for anyone interested in business civilization or in problems of social organization.

General Motors was founded in 1908 by one of the great members of the genus *Industrial genius.* W. C. Durant's style of operation, according to Sloan, was like that of any other charismatic type, whether in politics, religion, labor, or any other social movement. Like the better known Henry Ford, and perhaps more so, Durant succeeded because he combined a knowledge of automobiles with an ability to inspire those who commanded the necessary resources. Sloan places both Durant and Ford in the same category as men who, in his experience, had uncommon "vision, courage, daring, imagination, and foresight."[42] They were tremendous gamblers, as everyone knows, but more importantly they were what Sloan calls "personal types of industrialists; that is, they injected their personalities . . . as a subjective factor into their operations without the discipline of management by method and objective facts."[43] The operating styles of the two men differed considerably, but this may be owing as much to differences in their starting points as to those in their personal styles or preferences, because Mr. Ford owned his own system, whereas Mr. Durant pieced his together from preexisting parts.

In many ways Durant is a more interesting and remarkable type because he had to piece together so many different parts of what ultimately became a single organization. He started practically from scratch. He entered the automobile business in 1904 through the then failing Buick Motor Company. Some six years later, Durant had brought into the new General Motors nearly twenty-five companies, including eleven automobile companies, two elec-

---

[41] Alfred P. Sloan, *My Years with General Motors* (New York: Mac-Fadden, 1965).

[42] *Ibid.*, p. 4.

[43] *Ibid.*, p. 4.

trical lamp companies, and an assortment of parts and accessories manufacturers. Consolidation of such an empire involved many kinds of manipulations, some shady, some not. Most important it involved his leadership of extraordinarily intelligent and rational men. It involved the challenge of getting such men to put their faith, trust, and sacred fortunes into a visionary venture.

Life with Mr. Durant was extremely stormy and never stable. By September 1910, just two years after he had founded General Motors, Durant was forced out by an investment banking group responding to what seems to have been an overextended financial situation. Mr. Durant moved immediately into a new enterprise with Louis Chevrolet. By 1915 he had built Chevrolet into a nationwide organization, and by transferring his control over Chevrolet into General Motors stock, he had again become a major contender for control of General Motors. And despite the development of a block-Durant coalition between the take-over group and the du Ponts, in 1915 Durant regained control of General Motors. A wide open fight never materialized, because the bankers retreated in the face of a threat that Durant would expand his own stock holdings through an unprecedented proxy contest. Here again is another bold leadership trait that served him well during the period of creativity.[44]

This period of creativity was replaced by a period of consolidation and, as Sloan put it, "he could create, but not administer."[45] After having regained control and the presidency of the company, Durant turned directly to one of his adversaries, the du Pont family, and brought them into a collaborative arrangement with himself. Within a year Durant had convinced the du Pont people to such an extent that they were enthusiastically supporting his expansion. But quite soon this expansion led to disaster, and at the end of Durant's reign, General Motors was a managerial nightmare. Durant had carried his creation around in his hat, and such a giant could no longer rest easily there.[46] In order to consolidate,

[44] Most of this account will be found in *ibid.*, chaps. 1, 2, et passim.
[45] *Ibid.*, p. 4.
[46] See *ibid.*, p. 25.

new leaders were needed. Durant could not and did not survive the business slump of 1920, and on November 30 he resigned as president of General Motors. As Durant's eventual successor stated: "Mr. Durant's management methods let things get out of control."[47]

Durant's immediate successor was Pierre du Pont. During du Pont's essentially interim presidency, his eventual successor, Alfred P. Sloan, was assigned the job of studying the "concept of the organization." Sloan's work on the innards of General Motors was not mere technique and procedure, but a profound self-study, dealing with the organization in terms of its purposes, its goals, the missions of the separate parts of the organization, the financing, and so on. Sloan, following a three-year period of analyzing and studying the organizational aspects of General Motors, became its president in 1923 and continued in that capacity throughout the period of stabilization and maturation until 1946, when he retired to the post of chairman of the board.

It is unnecessary to go into the details of Sloan's presidency. Suffice it to say that it contrasted in the extreme from Durant's—in particular and meaningful ways. Sloan set out to create a collective leadership, and he set out to rationalize the chaos that had come from divisional autonomy within the parent organization. He centralized the fiscal operations and decentralized the production operation until General Motors became a model of balance between the center and periphery. He also systematized the relations among the specialties, including design, sales, advertising, and so on. One surprisingly difficult, but important, task was that of getting sufficient feedback from the periphery—particularly from the local dealers.

This period is almost exclusively characterized by efforts to articulate the over-all mission of the organization, putting everything into interrelated operational design, with every function properly apportioned and properly supervised. Sloan thus spans the periods from growth to stabilization in this colossal organiza-

[47] *Ibid.,* p. 38.

tion by first being its organization theorist and then its master bureaucrat. The bureaucratization of General Motors was certainly complete well before his retirement. And its consolidation as a concern willing to venture through relatively superficial model changes and technical improvements but to resist serious organization encroachments had occurred even earlier than bureaucratization.

The only major organizational change for General Motors in recent years has been its severance from du Pont; and this was an arrangement forced on it by the Supreme Court.

If students of business can be relied on, emphasis has been on finding and maintaining the closest possible fit among all the parts of the huge empire. Ultimately, it concerns the careful design of the individual as an organization man, through psychological testing, wife interviewing, career and salary plans. It includes seniority for workers, stock options for executives, and pensions for both. These, along with advances in the specialization of labor and human relations psychology, stabilize the organization by adjusting each individual to the other and by indenturing each to the organization. Departures from these intricate arrangements are indeed—from the standpoint of the organizations—irrational.

Capitalist Organization in Trade Associations

Trade associations were, like bigness and monopolization, another reaction to business dynamics. The trade association "movement" was most widespread at the turn of the century. It followed the most impressive building boom in the history of the world. The businessmen who formed such major trade associations as the National Association of Manufacturers in 1895 were reacting as a class to the same set of disequilibrating factors that motivated individual businessmen to form as large a single firm as they possibly could.

One might say that the trade association movement of the turn of the century and afterward was in effect a third stage of capitalism following the dynamic building phases. The first phase was very much as Adam Smith had described it in his theory of the market: a "small group" or individual entrepreneur stage that possessed the kind of dynamism and tolerance for uncertainty that the Smith market theory so well captures. In an important sense, the second phase of capitalism really begins with the founding of corporate forms of organization and the capacity to accumulate working capital far beyond the amounts that individual entrepreneurs could possibly amass. This second phase was a period of great charismatic leadership in organizational genius, best represented by what Josephson called "the robber barons." These and many others were the ruthless men who, like Durant, inspired people by the hundreds and then by the thousands to invest their personal wealth in some fantastic venture.

However, this dynamism tended to run down at two levels. One level was that of the individual firm itself, and at this level the result was very much like that of General Motors. But it was also true at the level of business as a class or a system. Many efforts to stabilize the business dynamic and to control the economic environment were made by the very same men who were building the gigantic corporations. But even if their pools and trusts had not been branded as illegal, these types of apparatus were relatively undependable, because agreements by specific firms to hold to the restraining contracts were extremely difficult to enforce. The very success of a multiple agreement to restrain trade led to irresistible pressures on individual members of the arrangement to violate the contract; the benefits of violating the contract were directly commensurate with the willingness of all other parties to the agreement to obey it. The sanctions for violating the contract were not very effective without government support. Thus once these arrangements were actually declared illegal, they were still more vulnerable, though they certainly did not cease to exist.

Since then the most successful device has been the trade association. Though it did not seek to restrain trade as completely as a pool or trust, its effect could be just as important, especially for the smaller firms that had no hope of becoming oligopolies or monopolies. The trade association was particularly attractive and effective in markets where there continued to be a great deal of dynamic competition.

It is widely reported that the trade association movement was a response to the initial success of the labor movement and that most trade associations existed for the purpose of union-busting. However, it is quite clear that that was only one and probably not the most important of the motivations. If we look at the actions of the trade associations from the time of their origin at the turn of the century, we find that only a small proportion of their activity was devoted to union problems. Most of their activity then and since has been directed to actual maintenance of the needs of the membership in the trade association. That is to say, the primary purpose of the trade association has been to stabilize relationships in the sector over which the trade association is organized. Labor costs and labor problems may crop up as a part of this, but they have been generally seen as part of the general market condition that is in need of stabilization. That is why trade associations have never found it very difficult to adjust to labor organizations once these have established themselves; more often than not there has been collaboration between the two, in order to maintain the stability of a given sector of the market.[48]

The culmination of the first major trade association movement was in the Federal Trade Commission Act and the Clayton Act, both passed in 1914. Insofar as the Sherman Act had been successful, government policies had had a disequilibrating effect on many sectors of industry. The trade association movement sought to remedy that without necessarily going back to a period of monopolies and trusts, which tended to work as much against the smaller firms as they did against the consumer. Thus, the primary objective of these two major trade regulation acts of the Wilson period was to curb the disequilibrating aspects of competition. This was done primarily by declaring certain business practices unfair competition, which, on analysis, turn out to be precisely the most dynamically competitive aspects of business. That is to say, the

[48] A more extensive assessment will be found in Chapter 3.

devices that were outlawed by the Federal Trade Commission and the Clayton Acts were the very devices that the most dynamic entrepreneurs were most likely to employ when trying to expand their share of the market. True, they outlawed such things as deceptive practices, fraud, and so on, which were already illegal under common law. But they also outlawed such competitive devices as price favoritism, rebating, advantages for certain buyers in order to gain in a certain region, special prices and rebates in a certain limited area in order to experiment with whether the product had an elastic or inelastic demand curve, and so on.

Such cutthroat competition devices were outlawed because they were supposedly the devices of entrepreneurs who intended to create monopolies in an otherwise competitive sector. But ironically, these devices are the devices of competition and are never used by successful monopolists. Sometimes they are used in order to maintain a monopoly position, but monopolies are created by other means, such as new inventions, new processes, or government policies. Thus, what trade regulation did after the advent of trade associations was to regularize business relationships and to create and perpetuate a government policy of restraint of competition. All sorts of theories emerge out of this period—such as "self-regulation," "partnership," and "business statesmanship." But, all the actions for which the trade association is responsible add up to an effort to harness and control the capitalist dynamic.

Thus, from the time of the emergence of the trade associations, capitalism took on new organizational form. In a sense it became politicized, but not only in the ordinary meaning of the term. Indeed, the trade associations immediately became important pressure groups; and that is politicization in the ordinary sense of the word. But the trade association represents a politicization of capitalism in an even more important sense. Relations among business firms and sectors came to be governed internally by the emergence of a business political system.

Here again, therefore, we find that resistance to change is less an ideological factor among businessmen than an organizational aspect of the life of business and organized capitalism. As with every other highly organized element in modern society, there are organizational characteristics that dictate organization maintenance over every other possible goal. And, as with the earlier cases of agriculture and labor, the phenomenon has very little to do with "goal displacement." Rather, the goals of the organization have become entwined with the needs of maintaining the organization, until the two have become indistinguishable and self-reinforcing. To change the one involves changing the other. Often in business this means avoiding risk; therefore to espouse with greater vigor the original goals of profit-making may not very well be possible. Profit maximizing might be played down in favor of profit-maintenance. But the goal of profit-making itself is never displaced. It simply becomes a part of organization maintenance, along with career and salary plans, stock options, and so on. Most changes in established businesses as in other established and organized sectors of the economy come from incremental changes in productivity.

The major innovations in the economy tend to come, as was demonstrated by Schumpeter long ago, through emergence of entirely new businesses based on some new invention, new technology, or new market. But this points to a far more general pattern: In any social situation nonincremental innovation tends to come from outside the established system or pattern of relationships. Innovations tend to be viewed by members of established systems as disequilibria, even as irrationality.[49] The alienated observer must turn to some reality and some theoretical model other than the group process, if he is to have a prayer of finding a way out of the very bondage of that group process.

[49] See Mannheim, *Ideology and Utopia* (New York: Harvest, n.d.), p. 199 ff.

2
Social Change: The Challenge to Pluralism in American Life

Modern U.S. society is not the society Madison envisioned as the solution to the problem of tyranny in a country of continental size. The highly organized groups that abound in our society seem to present a picture, not of dynamic equilibrium but of a society that is running down, a society in a state of decadence. But perhaps Madison's model has had its meaning altered as we have grown further away from his society.

Persistence versus Change

In providing us with a basis for a pluralist view, Madison spoke of factions; he said nothing about groups. And a faction is not a group. De Tocqueville also does not use groups in his formulation. In fact, he goes a long way to contrast the "principle of association" in the United States with what he himself calls "the permanent association," exemplified either by towns and cities established by law or by associations in Europe that "centralize the direction of their forces as much as possible and entrust the power of the whole party to a small number of leaders."[1] With Madison, he viewed pluralistic society as composed of large numbers of persons *in the process of forming groups,* rather than a society that is organized in groups. A fresh reading of de Tocqueville on voluntary associations gives a strong sense that what he had in mind as the genius of American politics was a peacetime version of the old Minutemen, poised to act on an issue at a moment's notice, but, until called, remaining private individuals engaged in their own selfish pursuits.

Factions, voluntary associations, and groups all belong to the same genus in almost any conceivable system of classification. But it seems extreme to call all of them groups. A faction seems to be a nascent group. But is that the same thing as a formed group? A faction is an effort to create a new power arrangement—a voting majority or something of the sort. A voluntary association is an effort to bring about a more direct resolution of an issue through the weight of numbers or focused attention. In both instances, the effort is itself the dynamic character of a political society. But is the collectivity the same, and is its impact on society the same, after it has become a group dedicated to its own maintenance and to the protection of those ends for which it is organized?

In 1954 a small group of graduate students at Yale became involved with Robert Dahl in a study of the community of Guilford, Connecticut. It was one of the earliest in a long line of power structure studies. In Guilford, a tiny New England town, we found at least 150 groups. Yet Guilford was one of the least dynamic societies one could find in the U.S. The existence of so many groups seemed only to ensure that few people would have time,

[1] Alexis de Tocqueville, *Democracy in America* (New York: Random House, Vintage Edition, 1955), vol. 1, chap. 12. See also vol. 2, chap. 5, where he contrasts the voluntary associations in the United States with the "permanent and compulsory association" of aristocratic communities.

energy, or inclination to form a "faction" or a "voluntary association" around some new and upcoming issue. This kind of pluralist
society, composed of organized groups, is static. It has little
political vitality. And it is in no way a meaningful antidote to the
problem of "mass society." Mass society, says Kornhauser, will
become mobilized unless there are numerous "intermediate
groups."[2] But a pluralist society composed of organized groups is
already mobilized. A mass society and a fully group-organized
society are two different instances of social attributes taken to their
logical extremes. The sooner we come to see both as undesirable
extremes, the better off we shall be.

All this anticipates the governing proposition of this book: The
difference between formed groups and groups in the process of
formation (nascent groups) is the difference between persistence
and change. A political society that is made up primarily of formed
groups will be a static society, and our society is static to the
extent that it is made up of formed groups and takes the formed
group as a virtue.

So significant is the factor of organization in our society that it
becomes, in one way or another, the identifying and unifying mark
of contemporary social science. Merton and many others speak of
functions and the self-maintaining capacity of organized life.
Easton and others speak of persistence and feedback. Truman and
a large body of the political science profession speak of equilibrium.
Nor can we find fault with them for this, for this is the nature of
modern society. Persistence is a dominant fact of modern life.
Modern social scientists are not conservative if they make organized
life their dominant concern. It is organized life itself that is conservative.

But where then does change come from? A society that is as
organized as ours loses much of its capacity for change. Yet ours
is also a society in which, at least so far, a great deal of change
has taken place. It is clear that the answer is not to be found in
groups and group relationships. It is useless to try to explain change

---

[2] William Kornhauser, *The Politics of Mass Society* (New York: The
Free Press, 1961).

with the precise variables and patterns with which we explain persistence.

The solution to this problem is perhaps to go back to the original inspirational texts, to take their original notion of the process of forming groups rather than that of formed groups, and then to look at phenomena of change rather than at phenomena of maintenance. We can then deal with pluralism without dealing with groups at all, by translating the notion of faction and voluntary association into the contemporary idea of *social movements* rather than into the contemporary idea of *groups*. The literature on social movements is almost as vast as that on groups. The phenomenon arises out of the same conditions of liberty and freedom, yet the implications and consequences could not be more different.

Social Movements: Toward an Alternative Model

Looking at society through the mechanism of social movements provides a worthy jolt to the political imagination. For several reasons, such a viewpoint in fact offers hope for considerable advance in political theory.

First, looking at movements rather than groups provides an entirely new slant on politics, because it unavoidably focuses on the processes of change rather than the processes of persistence. Through such a focus we may discover both the limits of the group system and a means of accommodating it, without abandoning it, to a broader, more balanced view of the way political society operates in advanced countries.

Second, the social movement is actually a way of looking systematically at groups. In a sense, we can take the social movement as a laboratory within which to study the group process. Not all groups began as social movements, and not all social movements congeal into groups. However, many of the most important groups began as social movements, and all groups possess most of the attributes and tendencies of social movements. It is the subtlety of the interrelations among these attributes that makes groups so difficult to study and the social movement such an attractive laboratory. In this sense, then, a social movement can be treated as a dramatic moment in the organization of interests, a phase through which all interests go if the people who share these interests wish to organize successfully around them in order to shape the environment in a systematic way.

Finally, with the first two points clearly in mind, the study of social movements may very well provide us with a basis for staging a massive critique of modern political processes without engaging in empty polemic and without merely picking at the nits of pluralist theories. We can take a good look at what worriers call "disorder," and we may find that it is a good deal more meaningful than the word implies.

Getting Organized

Any collective activity that involves more than a few people must be organized. But from the standpoint of the individual and of the society, getting organized presents certain dilemmas. For the efficiency of an organization is actually a measure of its resistance to other ways of organizing to do the same job or a related job. In economics the effort to organize might be considered one of "sunk costs." Organizing is an immense investment in time, emotion, and ego, as well as money.

In contemporary society the preorganized, or primitive, condition is a mass—any category of persons, whether that category is the result of conventional designation (consumers, women, stock purchasers) or the result of a definition by some observer (the radical right, an ethnic group, alienated students). What happens when such a mass seeks to convert itself into a meaningful social component?

The conversion of any mass into a group involves a significant increase in the frequency of interaction among the persons who share the attribute in question.[3] Close study of this conversion suggests that the increased interaction is two-dimensional. Persons who share a certain attribute discover that, for one reason or another, they have the attribute in common, and they seek one another out (1) through increasing the degree of mutual awareness and mutual personal identification or (2) through increasing their mutual functional identification—that is, what each might do for the other. The first dimension has been called integration. Informally, it is "groupness." The second dimension is thought of as differentiation, or "structuring."[4]

1. Integration is not a very abstract concept. It involves exchanges of names: Individuals seek to grow familiar with one another. In theory, such expanded interaction increases realization of common values and experiences. (If it does not, then no further effort will be made to get acquainted and form a group.) Expectations develop, involving the whole person, what he is like, what he is likely to react to, what will offend him, and so on. Sometimes this is a rather emotional matter; interaction may be at a totally nonverbal level whose expectations are expressed as simple loves and hates, satisfactions and frustrations. Following Tönnies, sociologists have called this kind of integration *Gemeinschaft,* loosely translated as "fraternity," or "community." At other times, but particularly after members of a mass have developed a notion of membership, the interactions are more rational,

[3] David B. Truman, *The Governmental Process* (New York: Knopf, 1951), p. 24: "It is the interaction that is crucial . . . , not the shared characteristic."

[4] For an example of sociological analysis of movements in which these two dimensions are taken implicitly as the primary functional prerequisites, see Joseph Gusfield, "Functional Areas of Leadership in Social Movements," reprinted in Barry McLaughlin, *Studies in Social Movements* (New York: The Free Press, 1969), pp. 481–482. Gusfield speaks of the "mobilizing function," which refers to reaffirmation of the goals and values of the organization and the building of membership commitments to the goals of the organization; he identifies the "articulation function," by which he means "linking the organization and its tactics to those of other organizations and to the larger society." For a related and highly suggestive parallel, see Gabriel Almond on "interest aggregation" and "interest articulation" in Gabriel Almond and James Coleman, eds., *The Politics of the Developing Areas* (Princeton, N. J.: Princeton University Press, 1960), introduction.

that is, capable of being verbalized. Integration is then based more on mutual awareness of what each member can gain or lose from another person and from his membership. This, again following Tönnies, is called *Gesellschaft,* loosely translated, "society."

Sir Henry Maine captured an essential aspect of this distinction in his observation that modernizing societies shift the predominant basis of integration from status to contract. Some groups, and even some whole societies, may remain integrated at the level of *Gemeinschaft.* Other groups, as in a big corporation, may begin as *Gesellschaft*-type organizations. In all organizations both elements are present, however, and they tend to be competitive. This is why on the paradigm (see Table 2–1) *Gemeinschaft* and *Gesellschaft* are treated as a dichotomy. There is always some element of both kinds of integration present, but that one or the other is likely to be dominant is significant.

2. The second dimension (the vertical one in Figure 2–1) also involves increased interaction among members of the mass. But the increase has to do with roles and functions, that is, with parts of each person rather than with whole persons. If integration involves intensified identification, *differentiation* involves increased interdependence. People learn to expect certain things of others, to rely on others to play certain rather specific roles and to perform certain specific tasks. The key aspect of differentiation is the division of labor; but differentiation also involves division of authority, division of tasks, division of time, division and allocation of resources and sequences, as well as division of jobs and skills. On the paradigm this complex bundle of interactions is treated as a single continuum broken into its high and low extremes. But the reader should constantly remind himself that this oversimplification is only for purposes of analysis; in reality differentiation involves several interrelated continua.

The paradigm (Table 2–1) is the result of a simple cross-tabulation of the two dimensions of organizational life. For example, what would be the most likely description of any collectivity whose members associated with one another through strong fraternal bonds but whose functional associations were quite rudi-

TABLE 2-1

Social Movements—A Paradigm

		Modes of Integration	
		Gemeinschaft (primary group)	*Gesellschaft* (secondary group)
Degree of Differentiation	Low	**Stage 1:** Spark of Life. Definition of issues; discovery of common irritants. Emergence of leader and cadre; leader serves as focal point, "symbol bearer." Enthusiasm, personal interchanges among followers, charisma among leaders.	**Stage 2:** Status to Contract. Expansion of issues, development and articulation of interests. Taking on new adherents; tangential relations more contractual. Succession of theoretic or entrepreneurial leaders and leadership functions. Disciples; sect to denomination. Systematization of charisma.
	High	**Stage 4:** The Group. Internalized norms. Established but informal leader-follower relations; bureaucratized at top, but loose below among members. Development of a representative process and the myth of majority rule. Limiting case: the totalitarian group, the *bund* of "order."	**Stage 3:** Jesus, Don't Come Back. From Paul to Peter; (denomination) to the church. Theoretic to bureaucratic leaders; articulation of organization doctrine with goals (operational codes). Full routinization of charisma. Limiting case: the bureaucracy.

mentary or "unstructured"? (Cell 1.) What could we say of any collectivity whose members were quite aware why they had joined but whose roles were still not very formalized? (Cell 2.) And so on.

To an extent, the analysis based on the paradigm is intended to lead toward a large and more comprehensive theory of organization. But its primary purpose here is the more modest task of trying to find a few regularities in group life that will help explain why groups tend to be so dynamic at first and so sluggish and contrary as they grow older.[5]

First Stage: Spark of Life

In Michelangelo's spectacular painting on the Sistine ceiling, God is about to create Adam. Their index fingers are pointed at each other, poised hardly an inch apart. Across that space one can almost see passing the mysterious spark that will begin all human life. Something like that must happen if a mass is to cross the threshold of organizational life. Some observers speak of this as the sudden discovery of common irritants. Others are struck by the emergence and definition of the issue or issues between the

[5] There is a strong developmental or evolutionary element suggested by the paradigm and throughout the analysis. Inasmuch as integration and differentiation are usually thought of as developmental, it is irresistible to conceive the interactions of the two as developmental also. However, an important exception is in order here. Though development, even orderly evolution, seems to be an attribute of the ultimate theory, the paradigm is not now constructed to present any necessary order among the stages. The cells are numbered and presented in that order here, but I would not be ready to formalize the ordering, not yet at any rate. So, not every group must move from stage 2 to 3 in order to confirm an underlying theory of development.

This clears the decks then to affirm more strongly what *is* intended here: The intimate interdependence among the parts of an organization, at each and every stage of development, constitutes the key factor in the analysis. The paradigm captures this and also the second key factor, that development, whatever its sequence, is not smooth and linear but "cornered" and critical. The move from any one stage to any other is likely to be abrupt, is likely to evoke a sense of crisis in the organization, and for these reasons is likely to be resisted. These are the tendencies, not the orderliness of the sequences, that may help explain the iron law of decadence.

emerging movement and society; still others speak of tangential interests and overlapping attitudes. But whatever it is called, it is that sensitive point where people find some basis of interaction—or else the mass will remain a mass.[6]

It is not the aim of this chapter to inquire in detail into the causes of movements and organizations; yet it might help define the character of stage 1 if certain typical causes were identified. First, of course, masses may initiate collective identity as a result of changes in the objective situation of the members. The aftermath of war and plight of depression are oft-cited examples. However, the objective situation need not move only downward to cause a movement. An upward change is just as likely to do so. Tocqueville once observed that the French found their position the more intolerable the better it became. Many others, including Durkheim, were struck by this. The proliferation of movements in the United States in the past decade or so, especially black movements, relates rather clearly to great prosperity. The point is that *any* disequilibrium can provide impetus for the conversion of masses into organizations.

Another spark of life stems from changes in ideology or values. Changes in values can cause movements if they lead to changes in the assessment of the objective situation, and this is true even if the actual situation has not changed at all. The spread of such ideas as Christianity, Islam, capitalism, and socialism obviously produced an impact quite separate from the situation in which they took root. On a far lower order of historical importance, the Vietnam War has changed little in the objective situation inside the United States, but conflict over the legitimacy of the war has led to a redefinition of many domestic values. And these changed values have in turn had a great deal to do with the spread of a movement mentality in the United States during the late 1960s.[7]

[6] See Truman, *Governmental Process,* chaps. 2–5, and Rudolf Heberle, *Social Movements* (New York: Appleton-Century-Crofts, 1951).

[7] See Neil J. Smelser, *Theory of Collective Behavior* (New York: The Free Press, 1963), chap. 3, esp. on "structural strain." See also Rudolf Heberle, *Social Movements,* esp. chap. 6.

But what happens once the mass has indeed crossed the threshhold into organizational life? Mere discovery of common destinies, common devils, or common disasters must be brought to deeper levels of intensity and must spread to larger numbers of people. The paradigm suggests that this rudimentary level is usually integrated emotionally (*Gemeinschaft*). During any conversion people tend to concentrate the greater part of their energies on that situation to the exclusion of all other concerns. But even so, some definition also must be going on, and this is why it seems so necessary to look at any organization, especially a movement, in terms of our two dimensions simultaneously.

The most fundamental act of differentiation is probably the division of labor between leaders and followers. But given the deeply emotional character of integration during the early life of the organization, that leadership is probably of a very special sort. The leaders must share with special intensity the fellow feeling that is creating the new primary group. But they must also function as a channel of communication. For the common symbols must be passed along as frequently and as intensely as possible, and face-to-face interaction is extremely inefficient beyond a few persons. That is why, during this early phase in the life of a movement, leaders must be highly charismatic.[8] And the larger the mass the more pronounced is the charismatic character of the leadership likely to be. At this extremely sensitive point, when a mass may not succeed in organizing at all, there is an urgent need for leaders who can function as symbol bearers, channels of communication, and emotional middlemen.

---

[8] Weber defines charisma as "an extraordinary power, as of working miracles or speaking many tongues, etc., said to be possessed by some of the early Christians." This notion has been generalized beyond the specifically religious to include all those who enjoy the reputation for special qualities—great demagogues, agitators, fanatics, prophets, etc. See Max Weber, *The Theory of Social and Economic Organization,* A. M. Henderson and T. Parsons, trans. (Oxford, 1947), pt. 3; see also Heberle, *Social Movements,* p. 131 ff., Renzo Sereno, *The Rulers* (New York: Praeger, 1962), p. 116 ff., and Eric Hoffer, *The True Believer* (New York: Harper & Row, 1951), p. 119 ff.

The emergence of a leadership with these characteristics tends in turn to convert the membership into a following.[9] As Mosca put it so well, "However exceptional the master's originality of vision, his strength of feeling, his aptitude for propaganda, those qualities are without avail if he does not succeed in founding a school before his material or spiritual death. . . ."[10]

Stage 2: Status to Contract

Some movements may remain in a rudimentary state, maintaining all the original passion, all the primitive relations to the symbols, the situation, and the leadership. Undoubtedly some movements have managed to spread and make significant changes in society without changing their original natures. However, as the paradigm suggests and most studies confirm, at some point the nascent group does begin to change, and with its maturation it begins to face crises of such importance that the very survival of the group or movement seems to be at stake.

If the movement spreads, new members join in droves, and they are simply not like the original members. Membership comes to be definable. The purposes of members and of the organization itself become clearer. Efforts must continually be made to maintain some clearly understood relationship between the members and the life of the organization. Even the original members must be reminded of their reasons for having joined. Sir Henry Maine encapsulated this development best in his formulation of the move from status to contract. To speak of the increasingly contractual relation of new members to the organization is simply to concretize the abstract notion of *Gesellschaft*.

At this stage (cell 2) there is not yet much differentiation. But even when the nascent group begins to "mature" there usually remains for a long time a "movement style," in which the mem-

---

[9] See Heberle, *Social Movements,* p. 132.
[10] Gaetano Mosca, *The Ruling Class* (New York: McGraw-Hill, 1931), p. 171.

bers get a great deal done quite spontaneously. There continues to be a great deal of room for creativity and inventiveness; necessary tasks are done even as members seem merely to be enjoying the experience of being together.[11] However, very early in the game—even before there is much self-conscious assignment of tasks—this spontaneity is overlaid with more and more self-consciousness.

Clearly, this can be a critical time in the life of a nascent organization. It brings on sudden stresses that the leaders and members must adjust to if the movement is to survive as an organization. Yet in adjusting, some always wonder whether the original purposes survived at all. The second stage is likely to be very much feared by the old guard. The spirit of conversion is lost. Dedication is doubted. "Were you with us before or after our successes, comrade?"

Such changes are likely to be more feared by the original leadership, which tends to be "exclusionary, desiring to limit the body of saints only to those full of grace."[12] And the reason is plain: A change in the membership requires adjustments in the behavior and functions of the leadership, just as it requires adjustments in the values and compensations of the old membership, Each expansion compels the leadership to make still further adjustments in both their behavior and the structure of the organization, and these adjustments may in turn put still further stresses on the leaders and the original hopes.

[11] I am grateful to Chicago graduate student, Jo Freeman, for teaching me about movement style. This notion is not intended to deny the importance of Lenin's cadre or vanguard. The larger the initial movement the more likely there is to be an effective vanguard of leadership from the beginning. Nevertheless, much of the daily activity is self-directive, and to such an extent that the top leadership might feel it to be a problem that has to be dealt with.

[12] John P. Roche and Stephen Sachs, "The Bureaucrat and the Enthusiast," *Western Political Quarterly* (June 1965), reprinted in Barry McLaughlin, *Studies in Social Movement,* p. 211: "this problem of membership has plagued social movements from time immemorial . . . ; suffice it to say that the struggle between the inclusionists and the exclusionists . . . inspired St. Augustine's polemics against the Donatists [just as it did] those of the Bevanites against Atlee. . . ."

The very concept of the old guard captures some of the flavor of the problem at this stage of development, which Mannheim may describe best of all:

Groups . . . in which the communal element prevails, may be held together by traditions or common sentiments alone. In such a group [*Gemeinschaft*], theoretical reflection is of entirely secondary importance. On the other hand, in groups which are not welded together primarily by such bonds of community life, but which merely occupy similar positions in the social-economic system [*Gesellschaft*], rigorous theorizing is a prerequisite of cohesion. Viewed sociologically this extreme need for theory is the expression of class society in which persons must be held together not by local proximity but by similar circumstances of life in an extensive social sphere.[13]

Others have looked specifically at what the change in basis of integration does to the functions and styles of leadership. As Hoffer has put it, "When the movement is ripe, only the fanatic can hatch a genuine mass movement."[14] But there comes a time when neither the incantations of the fanatic nor the sacred words of the charismatic will suffice. Original principles do not disappear; they become theories—systematic rationalizations of the organization in relation to its internal processes and external environments. And this means that the functions of the leaders will change accordingly.[15] It is unusual for the original leaders to survive the transformation from the first to the second stage, but those who do survive do so only by significantly changing their activities. Lenin survived, probably because he was a good, practical theoretician. Other charismatic leaders survive only by being relegated to ceremonial functions while the real power gravitates more and more to those who have control of the working principles. Jesus gives way to Paul and the Disciples, who maintain the mysteries but also write the texts and teach the applicable lessons. The sect becomes a denomination.[16]

[13] Karl Mannheim, *Ideology and Utopia* (New York: Harcourt Brace, 1936), p. 131.
[14] Eric Hoffer, *The True Believer*, p. 130.
[15] See esp. Mannheim, *Ideology and Utopia*, p. 131.
[16] See Smelser, *Theory of Collective Behavior*, p. 359 ff, and the citations there, esp. Troelstsch.

Martin Luther King provides one of the best contemporary examples of the problem of leadership transition and the failure to make it. Well before King's murder his organization, the Southern Christian Leadership Conference, had come to need something more than the evangelistic poetry and energy he so well provided. His inability to formulate applicable theory and policy for a truly national movement contributed to the weakening of his leadership in the entire civil rights movement. This in turn contributed to the serious fragmentation of the movement itself and the emergence of other leaders and other fragmentary movements, many based on principles diametrically opposed to those of Dr. King.

This period in the life of a movement is a time for propaganda and what the propagandist would call "the gradual persuasion and education of the masses." Rationalization of organizational goals and of appropriate member behavior become articulated as a single continuum of theory. In Christianity, for example, doctrine had to be extended from teachings about the afterlife, through social ethics and individual morality (how to reach the afterlife), to such organizational requisites as celibacy for the priesthood and confessional and dietary practices for the parishioners.[17] Theorists, entrepreneurs, intellectuals, all find themselves elevated to higher and higher positions in the developing organization. In our day the mimeograph machine has come to symbolize the transformation. As Mannheim put it, "a theoretical *Weltanschauung* has a unifying power over great distances."[18] Here Mannheim quotes Lenin: "Without a revolutionary theory there can be no revolutionary movement."[19]

Though the paradigm shows a very logical and distinct place for this second phase of development, and though many, like Mannheim, put special stress on the importance of this particular transitional phase, other observers tend to fuse it either with stage 1 or

[17] See Mosca, *The Ruling Class*, pp. 190–193.
[18] Mannheim, *Ideology and Utopia*, p. 131.
[19] Quoted in *ibid.*, p. 131.

stage 3. Hoffer, for example, sees the founders of movements as being simultaneously prophets and theorists.[20] The stronger tendency is to treat theorizing as an organizational role akin to other roles played by the organization men and bureaucrats of the third stage.[21]

But whether or not there is a distinct and separate "second stage," the point is that there is an important moment in the life of an organization when its needs shift away from getting the action started. Between charisma and the full routinization of charisma there seems to be an important link we might call the "systematization of charisma." The cause and its history have to be explained in terms of the everyday behavior of the members. Someone has to make a concordance between the grand ideals, poetically expressed by the prophets in the beginning, and the not-so-poetic strategies that the maturing organization requires. Sometime during this rationalizing phase, the organization turns a critical corner. The point of change may be more distinct and more critical for some organizations than for others, but, distinct or not, everything tends to need adjusting and changing all at once.

Stage 3: Jesus, Don't Come Back

The movement style can bring any organization a long way toward the achievement of its goals. In some ways, spontaneous allocation of tasks is actually enhanced by the first efforts of the theorists to articulate goals and rationalize strategies. But at some point there begins a more pronounced differentiation. More things must be done by more people. The organization has to be designed so that there is a certainty that some functions will be performed and sooner or later this allocation of duties can no longer be

[20] Hoffer, *The True Believer*, p. 119 ff.
[21] For examples, see Roche and Sachs, "Bureaucrat and Enthusiast"; and Herbert Blumer, "Social Movements," in McLaughlin, *Studies in Social Movements*, p. 12 ff.

accomplished informally. There comes a point when the boss can no longer run the business out of his hat. Whether he dies or retires, he will probably not be replaced. His job will probably be broken up into several tasks, formalized, and turned over to several different people.[22] With increased size comes differentiation, formalization of doctrine, formalization of leadership functions and selection, the ordering of membership roles, and even the regularizing of relations with the outside world.

This articulation and formalization of parts may be the major transformation in the life of the developing organization. Perhaps the most dramatic shift takes place in the leadership. Though many leaders may survive the transformation from first to second stage, survival from the second to third stage is much less likely. For the requirements of leadership move from the theoretic to the bureaucratic. This is the managerial takeover. Political man emerges.

Other things change, too, and in parallel fashion. Doctrines become more narrowly translated through application. Procedures become important: Rules must be fashioned, roles and statuses must be ascribed and continually adjusted to fit new situations. It is easy to see why the old leadership and the original members feel out of place.

Even the goals themselves undergo a transformation. Some have called this process "goal displacement," as though the movement tends eventually to forget what it was about.[23] This is of course

[22] See Alfred P. Sloan, *My Years with General Motors* (New York: McFadden, 1965); also Rinehard Bendix, *Work and Authority in Industry* (New York: Harper & Row, 1963), esp. chaps. 2, 4, and 5; for parallel developments in management and labor, see C. Wright Mills, *White Collar* (New York: Oxford University Press, 1951), ch. 5 et passim.

[23] This notion probably originates with Robert Michels, *Political Parties* (New York: Dover, 1959 [First published English trans. 1915]) pp. 366–367: "As the organization increases in size, the struggle for great principles becomes impossible . . . [E]very struggle on behalf of ideas within the limits of the organization is necessarily regarded as an obstacle to the realization of its ends, an obstacle, therefore, which must be avoided in every possible way."

a distinct possibility. But the greater likelihood is that the movement will not lose its original goals but will organize and interpret them in ways adapted to its organizational needs. "Goal articulation" may be a better notion. In the United States we like to look back at the "intentions of the framers" and find their guidance for totally unanticipated issues. Some organizations carefully redefine and parcel out their goals as specific organization "incentives."[24] But whatever happens, actual displacement seems to be the exception. The rule seems to be that goals are somehow maintained but lose a little something in being translated into organizational requirements.[25]

The limiting case of these organizational developments is bureaucracy—that is, if *Gesellschaft* and differentiation were both pushed to their absolute extremes, every member would have a clearly ascribed organizational role and function, coupled with a quite rationalized and conscious relation to each fellow member. Leadership and doctrine would be strictly matters of "scientific management." No movement and few organizations of any sort except manufacturing concerns and military forces ever come close to reaching this stage. But even short of that extreme, the movement has moved far indeed from its original state of spontaneity, zeal, and simplicity. In fact, the nascent group does not have to have a great deal of history before it comes face to face with the dilemma dramatized by Dostoevski when, in Ivan's dream, the Inquisitors determined that a Second Coming could be the worst thing that had ever happened to the Church. Had the Church given up on Christian goals, or had they reached a point where the unadulterated simplicity of Jesus's doctrines and management had become ridiculously inappropriate for the large, international

[24] See Mancur Olson, *The Logic of Collective Action;* and James Q. Wilson and Peter B. Clark, "Incentive Systems: A Theory of Organizations," *Administrative Science Quarterly* (1961), 129–166.

[25] One of the best case studies of this translation will be found in Michael Parenti's "The Black Muslims: From Revolution to Institution," *Social Research,* Summer 1964.

Christian "movement"? To summarize, the movement is no longer a movement when the leadership can get together and say: "Now your office will give us some charisma, and our office will provide some more doctrine, the other bunch will give us circuses, and the members will provide us with bread."

Stage 4: The Group

The movement has become something of a group as soon as it has some structure, history, and social integration. But this fourth stage is concerned with mature groups in which the norms and goals of the organization have been internalized by the members—where, for purposes of the organization, it is a way of life. For this to be the case, the nascent group must have gone through a great deal of group development, whether it has precisely followed the stages of the paradigm or not.[26]

Some developing organizations go the route of business, political machines, government agencies, and the military: They remain in the third stage by continuing to ascribe functions to each member —in other words, they become bureaucratized. But most organizations, especially those that specifically began as movements, do not attempt bureaucratization. Instead, they bureaucratize at the very top, establish a few rules to order member relationships, and then depend on these rules and a lot of "primary group" attachments to carry out functions and maintain cohesion.

This is not so stable a situation as the more bureaucratized organization, and as a consequence two things tend to happen. One is the extreme case, the formation of the totalitarian group, or *bund*. This is really an effort to gain a solution through social integration rather than through differentiation. It involves intensification of social relations and the incorporation of more and more of the member's world into the organization (to reduce conflicting pressures of time or other goals). This is why the word "totalitarian" is appropriate for the limiting case. And thus, integration,

[26] See Karl Mannheim, *Ideology and Utopia,* pp. 141–143.

like differentiation, can be a way of maintaining the group and eliminating instability.[27]

The other, and far more typical, tendency is oscillation. That is to say, once the organization is fully formed its structures remain fairly loose, and its goals and internal rules are meaningful but never fully articulated. The organization is therefore in a continual state of adjustment with its internal processes and its environment. But this solution is not ideal, because each oscillation tends to involve each and every element of the organization. Let us now see how this very oscillation explains the iron law of decadence.

Groups as True Systems

Only by reviewing the intimate interrelationships among the parts of a developing organization can we begin to appreciate the character of group life and the fundamental difference between formed and nascent groups. The most striking aspect of the analysis is the degree to which the reality behaves like the model. The paradigm was a logical contrivance for closing off a system of analysis. But the analysis in turn suggests that groups are almost as closed a logical system as the paradigm itself. Every collectivity is a system to some extent. Even a group as loosely defined as a nation has a number of highly interrelated parts. But of all collectivities the organized group probably comes closest to being a closed system—as measured by the extent to which a change in one element affects all other elements in the organization. When groups are compared to neighborhoods, communities, even peak associations, these latter seem very loosely structured indeed.

What this means is that we get a multiplier effect. Every change becomes magnified by its reverberation throughout the organization. Almost any change of status can become a crisis, and the tacticians of the formed organization must be very watchful for

[27] See Maurice Duverger, *Political Parties* (New York: Wiley, 1954), p. 119 ff.

the seemingly unrelated events that may bring on the crisis for their entire regime. Organizations face a terrible dilemma. Being so interrelated, they face tremendous stresses that only greater organizational efforts can solve; yet at the same time, such intensified organizational effort renders the organization all the more interrelated and in need of further controls.[28]

Owing to their highly interrelated parts, mature groups are always in a state of oscillation. But the oscillation involves the bumping of all the parts against one another in an intense and roughly predictable fashion. That is to say, any disequilibrium affects the very structure of the organization to such an extent that it may very well repeat in great part its original formative stages. A sudden success, for example, may bring about a sudden influx of new members. The response we may then get is a reaffirmation of the organization doctrinal structure more characteristic of either stage 2 or stage 3. In trying to capture this phenomenon, Lasswell draws on a notion formulated by Michels, the "accordion rhythm" generated by the interplay of permeability and solidarity.[29] To Lasswell, this is a far more important factor than age in the life of a group. As he puts it, "the changing equilibrium among the significantly interacting variables has resulted in periods of 're-vitalization' and 'decay' (to use biological metaphors); or to speak more precisely, periods of relative stress on principled interests have reappeared more than once."[30]

In sum, the intimate interrelation among the parts of the organization pressures its members to avoid and prevent disequilibria. Stress on system maintenance is unavoidable. It is not a mere derivative of goal displacement. Neither is it a mere variant of the old idea of Michels that members are naturally conservative and prefer to keep things as they are. It is something still more profound. Conservatism is literally sown into the nature of organiza-

---

[28] See Joseph R. Gusfield, "The Study of Social Movements," *International Encyclopedia of the Social Sciences* (1968), p. 448.

[29] Harold Lasswell and Abraham Kaplan, *Power and Society* (New Haven: Yale University Press, 1950), p. 36.

[30] *Ibid.*, p. 43.

tion itself. In this sense, we can say that formed groups are inherently conservative regardless of the nature of the goals of the organization or the predispositions of its members.

Getting Change—Despite Groups

The history of the United States is not merely one of mutual accommodation among competing groups under a broad umbrella of consensus. The proper image of our society has never been a melting pot. In bad times it is a boiling pot; in good times it is a tossed salad. For those who are *in*, this is all very well. But the price has always been paid by those who are *out,* and when they do get in they do not always get in through a process of mutual accommodation under a broad umbrella of consensus.

However, equally unbalanced the other way is the new revisionism, the theory of mea culpa, namely, that U.S. history is one of repression and violence. Though there has been a great deal of both repression and violence, these seem rather to have been the spillover of some more profound subterranean process. A study of social movements suggests an alternative explanation, one that is not at all a synthesis of the two extreme positions but a third, quite different explanation.

Any political theory in the United States—moral or empirical—must begin with the recognition that our political system is almost perfectly designed to maintain an existing state of affairs—any existing state of affairs. This kind of political system was probably miraculously appropriate for our heterogeneous society. The Constitution alone—with its system of representation, separation of powers, federalism, bicameralism, judicial supremacy, and the Bill of Rights—gave an almost unassailable position to established minorities. The system favored established minorities all the more precisely because it worked by majority rule. As one observer put it, our system is so designed that only a determined and undoubted majority could make it move. This is why our history is replete with social movements. It takes that kind of energy to get anything close to a majority.

Our system is uniquely designed for maintenance. But if the constitutional system and the established support groups explain the amazing persistence and adaptability of our politics, quite evidently the other half of the explanation, that which explains change, lies outside the system—outside established institutions and organized arrangements. Such a relationship between the whole system and those elements that form in opposition to it can on occasion be violent, but this violence is fall-out and not essence. The essence lies in the relationship itself, between elements of the organized system and an evanescent but momentarily brilliant movement. Change comes, therefore, neither from the genius of the system nor from the liberality or wisdom of its supporters and of the organized groups. It comes from new groups or nascent groups—social movements—when the situation is most dramatic. New or nascent groups arise out of social pathologies and seek to respond to these pathologies. Old groups represent the cold remains of earlier pathologies now either passed by or actually resolved. Movements can succeed or fail; they can disappear and affect nothing thereafter, or they can persist, effect a change, and then defend the system and the changes that they help to effect. A successful movement eventually is a confirmation of an iron law of decadence. But it provides the society with a great deal of energy before that effect takes place. The good democrat should try to foster new groups and should distrust old groups. The wise democrat should always expect to be betrayed by the minorities he supports.

Consider briefly how the contrasting processes work. When a formed group interacts with another such group or with the government, the results overwhelmingly tend to be incremental. Too great a departure from the status quo would affect the actual internal structure of the group by changing the environment that the group has helped build; part of this environment has been incorporated into the very structure of the group. A great departure, therefore, threatens the existence of the group. Moreover, to behave other than in a bargaining and incremental way—that is, to seek gains that would exact too great a price for the adversary to pay—would violate the rules that groups have worked out as extensions of their needs for equilibrium. This is the "interest-group liberalism" that has become, as I have argued in *The End of Liberalism,* the prevailing political ideology in the United States. So influential has it been that it now even has its own jurisprudence, which technicians call the delegation of power to administrative agencies.[31]

This elevation to ideology has made it all the more difficult to bring about substantial change through politics. For, if groups are already overwhelmingly committed to the maintenance of an existing arrangement, they cannot help but be more effective when it becomes a virtue to work through the group process. And when government policy delegates power to administrative agencies, government is quite profoundly plugging itself into the interest-group system. Government agencies tend to stabilize the social process by establishing routines from which it is very difficult to depart. They further stabilize the social process by their tendency to recognize only those forces that are already stable and known quantities.

Now contrast this with the way new or nascent groups, especially social movements, operate. When movements act on the government or any of its parts, there tends to be action with very little interaction—that is, very little bargaining. But this is not violence, though the violation of some group rules by social movements may make it appear so. The effect of the movement is of another sort altogether: *The demands and activities of a movement tend to activate the mechanisms of formal decision-making.* Group *inter*action through bargaining is quite literally a move to "keep the dispute out of court." The old epigram, "What's a constitution among friends?" applies to the group process. But when leaders refuse to bargain, other rules apply. The rules are: confrontation,

[31] See also Chapter 3.

debate, formulation, voting, policy-making, and ultimately a decision that may require forceful imposition of a new policy on the society. But examine those words and those rules. *They define the formal democratic process.* A democratic government is inconceivable without full coercive imposition of laws democratically arrived at. Thus, in a very profound sense, new or nascent groups, without necessarily intending to, tend to hold a democratic system to its own pretensions.

Violence is, therefore, not the only alternative to bargaining. When the contestants cannot or will not compromise their demands, they do not necessarily encourage violence unless they want violence. They can cast lots or flip a coin. Or they can consult a seer. Or, they can demand a vote among all contestants and their followers. They can go to court, or agitate to change public opinion. Most established groups and government leaders abhor such a situation, because it gets out of hand; or the results are unpredictable; or the feedback onto the system itself can be damaging to established leadership patterns, organization patterns, and norms. But this is surely what Schattschneider had in mind in his brilliant essay on the "scope of conflict" and the consequences of seeking to expand it. As he put it:

the scope of conflict determines its outcome . . . There has indeed been a long-standing struggle between the conflicting tendencies toward the privatization and the socialization of conflict . . . A tremendous amount of conflict is controlled by keeping it so private that it is almost completely invisible . . . on the other hand, it is . . . easy to identify . . . ideas contributing to the socialization of conflict. Universal ideas in the culture, ideas concerning equality, consistency, equal protection of the laws, justice, liberty, freedom of movement, freedom of speech and association and civil rights tend to socialize conflict. These concepts tend to make conflicts contagious; they invite outside intervention in conflict and form the basis of appeal to public authority for redress of private grievances.[32]

---

[32] E. E. Schattschneider, *The Semisovereign People* (New York: Holt, Rinehart & Winston, 1960), pp. 7–8.

Movements from the left and from the right tend to be activated around these broader concepts, and provide a certain amount of contagion until late in their growth, when they too articulate their demands into narrower interests that the system can incorporate.

Ironically, this should emerge in the form of laws with clear legal integrity, for older groups can articulate their demands clearly enough to provide legislators with real help in framing clear legislation with clear guidance for administrators. But in actuality laws become worse. This is because established groups do not seek good legislation which, while favoring themselves, is applicable and clear to all. Instead old groups seek broad delegations of authority, so that government policies can be converted into resources that can help stabilize the internal group processes.

Activation of the formal mechanisms of decision-making as a response to contagion means voting, debate, and in general more decisions openly arrived at. It means a Congress that is more rather than less involved in real legislation. It means the enunciation of decisions that are clear enough to guide administrators. This is a tremendous contrast to the results of a bargaining process, where every effort is made to avoid clearly enunciating what the decision really is, and every effort is made to pass along the application of these laws to lower and lower levels where there is less and less visibility.

In *The End of Liberalism* I referred to the result of the bargaining process as "policy without law." Policy without law plugs into the system of interest groups, and everything about it is innately conservative. This analysis of group politics and social movements reinforces the policy analysis in *The End of Liberalism*. There I tried to show (1) how limited is the capacity of big government to bring about any important change and (2) how effective government really is when it seeks to maintain a given status quo. The study of social movements makes it all the more clear, at least to me, that government's capacity to change things is really limited to its use of positive law—that is, to its willingness to directly and coercively use the legitimate powers of the state on society in a way that is unmistakably clear to all. Ironically, the above describes the rule of law, which in the past generation has been associated with conservatism. Yet, this rule of law is the very thing that most social movements seek. Governments in the United States—federal, state, and local—have never moved with greater certainty or with greater effectiveness than when pushed by movements. And governments never move more vaguely and ineffectively, and never resist change so adroitly, than when guided by needs as defined by groups in a group bargaining process.

Despite a long history of movements—and one can appreciate their frequency best by looking at state and local history—Americans are nonetheless fearful of them and their abuses. Yet, safeguards against such abuses are built into our system. In addition to the constitutional safeguards against false or temporary majorities, there are also the usual criminal penalties for damages to property or persons that result from the actions of overzealous members of movements. The problem of movements in this country is not violence, but that the movements so quickly deteriorate into defensive groups.

Law and Disorder

A nation that is in need of stability is also in need of change. It follows that such a nation needs law and *dis*order. Yet, this is almost the opposite of the needs as expressed by policy-makers today. For purposes of future reform, disorder means the establishment of a norm—or I should say the reestablishment of the norm—that chaos is better than a bad program.

This is really what I meant when I spoke of juridical democracy in *The End of Liberalism*. I have been misunderstood on this point, for many colleagues have gotten the impression that I was looking to the Supreme Court to solve all our problems. It has been through the study of social movements that I have been able to set the matter straight, at least for myself, concerning rule of law and juridical democracy.

A bad program is a government response to an urgent demand that expresses the appropriate sentiments (for example, "put an end to poverty") but does not direct the coercive powers of the state clearly and effectively toward the pathology that activated the demand. Because the pressure is on, and good liberals feel they must have the program, they formulate it vaguely, delegate great discretion to the administrator, and expect him to work out the actual program in cahoots with all contestants. That is what I meant by "plugging into the group process." But meanwhile, the energy behind the demands that go into the enactment is bought off, and the discovery that it is bought off usually comes too late to do anything about the program. This buying off is relatively easy, because new and inexperienced leaders are simply ignorant of what they are in for when they interact with governments and politicians. In this manner, a premature, vague government response in a bad program is far worse than no government response at all.

Consider what happens when there is greater delay in the response. If there is no government response, or if the Supreme Court, through the powers to declare vague legislation unconstitutional, voids a bad program, the movement behind the demand continues to maintain its energy and its pressures. It persists and grows, and perhaps even improves on the formulation of its demands. Ultimately, if things are allowed to drift, and for a period of time chaos prevails, we are far more likely to get clear effective legislation than if we allowed Congress to respond by taking the bait off the hook and throwing it immediately down into the bowels of the administration. This is why I have argued that the power of the Supreme Court to declare broad delegations unconstitutional is perhaps the most important revolutionary force available to us. I did not mean to say that the court itself legislates or in any other way affects the revolution. The court does more legislating now by filling in the vagueness left by Congress. The role of the Supreme Court in preventing bad actions serves to set in train or

to maintain in force the movement energies that are acting from
without on the government.

The most important recent illustration is that of the civil rights
movement. During the early 1960s the movement had become an
overwhelming force in American life. Its morality was contagious,
and its size was becoming politically irresistible. But as the demands expanded from Southern problems to national problems,
the most important government response was the war on poverty.
This response could not have been better designed to kill the civil
rights movement and to protect existing relationships than if that
had been the original goal. The war on poverty left almost completely intact the national pattern of racism. It set up a program
that expressed hope that relief for the poor would be coordinated
at local levels. But the broad delegation of power to local levels
removed this policy process entirely from the focus of the large,
national movement. This meant transfer of the conflict from the
focus of the national movement down to a multiplicity of points
where the force of the movement would be lost through dispersion.

This process converted the revolutionary moral force of the
civil rights movement to a geographically segmented, economically
defined, and negotiable set of goals, around which locally oriented,
well-organized groups could form for purposes of negotiation. The
1950s movement for social justice was lost during the 1960s; it
was given over to a set of negotiable and administrable goals. All
that seems to be left of the national movement now is a dead
martyr and the rhetoric of black withdrawal, which plays directly
into the hands of the status quo ante by leaving completely untouched the established patterns of racist operation, including the
patterns of the two major political parties. On the sidelines, intensi-
fying their rhetoric through the forge of frustration, are the black
nationalists and separatists, on the one side, and the Wallacists and
other white nationalists and segregationists, on the other side. And
now it comes to pass that, despite their basically antilibertarian
sentiments, the so-called extremists may provide the only available
energy for real change.

It is in this sense, then, that rule of law rather than rule by delegation is an essential prerequisite of effecting lasting social change by deliberate, public means. In the past I have often referred to juridical democracy as a desirable variant of democracy. I am now coming to the conclusion that it is democracy itself. Properly understood, democracy *is* juridical, or it will not remain democratic or vital very long. Borrowing the term "law and disorder" is simply a way of putting the same thing into the context of social movements and other new groups that provide the most important means by which governments will formulate clear rules of law rather than vague delegations of power. In operation, this would mean that the primary obligation of a government is the relatively negative one of protecting civil liberties. This may involve something of a risky embrace of some unsavory wrongheaded movements, but a government that has achieved as much stability as ours is all the more in need of the feedback that large dynamic new groups can give it. Government can no more afford repression of these demands than it can afford the destruction of all its computers.[33]

[33] See Chapter 8 for further arguments along these lines.

PART II

FREEDOM *FROM* ASSOCIATION: CIVIL LIBERTIES AND THE FAILURE OF GOVERNMENTS

3

Decentralization: To Whom? For What?

In a time of great change, social movements present governments with new agendas and new urges to respond directly to society. Democratic governments are usually responsive, and U.S. governments are probably more responsive than most. But not all responses, even when sincere and meaningful, are equally productive; certain types of responses are in fact counterproductive.

Decentralization has become a fashionable mode of response. Yet there is little assessment of the methods and consequences of decentralization. If there were, there might be less propensity to favor it. Though it is understandable that Americans find the notion of decentralization attractive, there are strong reasons for being skittish about it. The most important of these is that decentralization tends to plug government into the interest-group system. Thus, during a time of great change like the present, decentralization, in effect, commits government to system maintenance just when it is trying to be, or at least trying to appear to be, on the side of change. To the many movement leaders who were educated to favor decentralization the outcome of decentralized policies ultimately begins to look like a gigantic stab in the back. In reality it is a stab in the front.

This chapter first appeared in *Midway* 9, no. 3 (Winter 1969). Copyright © 1969 by the University of Chicago Press.

Why Decentralization?

Americans are by tradition, habit, culture, and ideology fearful of power. Yet they see power only in certain places and not in others. They are prepared to defend themselves against certain kinds of power, but against other kinds of power they provide themselves with no safeguards whatsoever. The primary source of power to Americans—and therefore the direction against which they orient their safeguards—is the state. For more than a century after its founding, the Constitution of the United States was written and interpreted so as to prevent as effectively as possible the development of a strong state. The very word "state" tended to be replaced with such euphemisms as "government" and "the public sector," as if to avoid development of undue respect toward *l'état*.

Eventually *l'état* did expand, so that by the middle of the twentieth century the public sector equaled proportionately that of any of the Western European and Commonwealth democracies. But even after the expansion the Americans never ceased worrying about it. Each stage in government expansion came only after lengthy and elaborate constitutional debates in Congress and in the courts.

Moreover, each expansion of government power was accompanied by expansions in the mechanisms of representation. The first expansions of federal power, between 1888 and 1892 and between 1910 and 1914, were accompanied by spectacular social movements—populism and progressivism—each of which was strongly oriented toward enhanced representation. Their goals included congressional reform, direct election of senators, reform in methods of nominating candidates for public office, adoption of the secret ballot, and so on. Further expansions of government before and during the Woodrow Wilson administration were accompanied by further dramatic reforms in Congress, amending the Constitution to admit female suffrage, drastic reforms in the system of balloting, and major reforms in the structure of local government. During the New Deal period, the doctrine of "interest representation" became a dominating force in American political thought. The corporativist structure of the famous National Recovery Administration (NRA) is but one small example of the effort of political leaders to extend representation as a safeguard against the extension of the state. Since Roosevelt, the expansion of the state has been regular rather than by revolution—and the expansion of representative devices has been equally regular. Interest representation continues to be seriously demanded in the United States even as demands for it are declining in Europe. Significant advances have been made in suffrage and in methods of nomination. Even more significant reforms have taken place in methods of apportioning population in election districts.

But the state has not merely expanded; its expansion has taken on newer forms that may not be met at all by just expanding the mechanisms of representation. Americans, for example, have always looked with some consternation at the degree to which central state administration enters into private processes in the Western European democracies. The decrees and prefects in France, the aristocratic civil servant governing by discretion in England, the aloof civil servant governing by routine in Germany, the apolitical bureaucracies with their benevolent ombudsman in Sweden all seem too heavy-handed. Etatism has negative connotations in the United States because it means administrative intervention. Yet administration has also inevitably and unavoidably expanded in the United States, and it has excited all sorts of efforts to "solve the problem."

The latest cry is for decentralization. Related cries are for interest representation, cooperation, partnership, and creative federalism by the old left and for participatory democracy and community action by the new. All these cries are related; their aim is to find some means of conserving the creative, directive power of the state without losing the grip of localized popular control on that power. Inasmuch as these cries are inappropriate, all reforms responding to them are self-defeating.

Resistance to the development of centralized, bureaucratized administrative structures in the public sector is a policy on which most American liberals tend to agree with American conservatives. There has been an almost permanent consensus among political leaders in the United States in favor of expanding the state while retarding expansion of centralized, formal administrative intervention in private affairs. American trade unions have consistently opposed federal intervention in collective bargaining once the collective bargaining process was established. Farmers have been traditionally in favor of state intervention, but only on the basis of various forms of "cooperation." Most new social programs of the last decade have resulted at one and the same time in a large net expansion of state power and an incredibly intense effort to avoid giving the impression that there has been a net increase in bureaucratic power.

This concern for administrative power in the public sector has been matched by a singular lack of concern for the same thing in the private sector. There may be a large body of criticism concerning the overcentralization of capitalist wealth. There may be widespread recognition that some safeguards must be erected against this kind of "economic power." However, criticisms are rarely directed at the extent to which the private sector is now governed by an administrative state.

Decentralization to Whom?

The rise of the private administrative state began early and has been dramatic. For example, in less than half a century, between 1900 and 1950, administrative employees in the United States increased from less than 6 percent to nearly 25 percent of all industrial employees. These rates are comparable to those of Great Britain and Sweden. According to Reinhard Bendix, the rate of increase has been lower in Germany (from 5 percent to nearly

12 percent), and considerably lower in France (a static level of about 12 percent).[1] The latter two cases are particularly significant, because these two countries are known to have had the largest and most authoritative state apparatus. This suggests that the quantum of administrative need is about the same in all industrial states. The bureaucratization of the private sector is less understood in the United States, but its existence and its influence on private life are undeniable. Many an American giant corporation had a five-year plan before the concept was invented in the Soviet Union. Since 1956 white-collar workers in the United States have out-numbered blue-collar workers, suggesting the extent to which work and workers have been reduced to shuffling papers, handling routines, and supervising the conduct of others.

A more direct view of the private sector in modern industrial society is the trade association. It is a slightly extreme case of the typical. Thus it is a good introduction to the realities of politics after decentralization.

The trade association is basically an administrative structure whose quintessential mission in life is to regularize relations among potential competitors in the same industry, trade, or economic sector. In history and in theory, the law of the commercial market-place is competition. The trade association seeks to replace this with an administrative process.

Trade associations have been widely misunderstood, much to their own advantage in public relations. Social scientists tend to treat them as a form of interest group or pressure group, suggesting that the trade association is primarily a category of political activity. Within this rubric the trade association is merely a means of efficient representation of certain economic interests. This means, of course, that the trade association is a good thing insofar as there are always many trade associations, each representing distinct economic interests. Under such conditions no concern need be given to life within any of the respective associations.

---

[1] Reinhard Bendix, *Work and Authority in Industry* (New York: Harper & Row, 1963), chap. 4.

It is true that Washington and every state capital and city hall abound with trade associations and their political representatives, the lobbyists. However, political activity is only marginal and occasional with any trade association. First, there are thousands of issues confronting the legislatures of the country in any given year, and only very few of these issues will be salient to any one trade association. On public housing, for example, the National Association of Home Builders is intensely active; but new public housing legislation is not even an annual affair.

Second, political activity is a functional specialization inside each major trade association—a special responsibility that is assigned to one bureau among many bureaus inside the association. Meanwhile, the other bureaus are busy making their respective contributions to the other administrative responsibilities of the association. These responsibilities include research and development or subsidies therefor, information on pricing and costs, market research, joint advertising campaigns and other promotions, collection and dissemination of political information, and information regarding civic duties.

The population of trade associations began to mushroom during the late nineteenth century and was given special impetus during and after World War I. From the few guilds and rate bureaus existing as late as 1850, the trade association effort to formalize economic relations expanded until, in 1940, when an official census was taken, there were at least 12,000 national, state, and local trade associations. More than a quarter of these were national or international in scope.[2] No recent census has been taken, but there is no reason to expect that the number or importance of trade associations has declined. It is probable that no production or service facility in the nation exists without a trade association to control the behavior of its members. Single businesses of more

<hr />

[2] Cf. Donald C. Blaisdell, *American Democracy Under Pressure* (New York: Ronald Press, 1957), p. 59, and citations; see also E. E. Schattschneider, *The Semisovereign People* (New York: Holt, Rinehart & Winston, 1960), p. 31.

than modest size usually find it desirable to belong to several such associations.

If trade associations are primarily not political but administrative animals, neither are they the mere expressions of centralized and oligopolized economic sectors. The fact is that the more decentralized and potentially competitive sectors and industries need the trade associations and their administrative functions most of all. Where the number of firms is greater, the fear of competition is stronger, the need for research and marketing information is greater, and the need for systems of recruiting trained personnel and sharing the results of research and technological advances is far greater. Such services are often provided from within by the giant corporations, but among the smaller operations they are provided solely by trade associations. Thus, many of the most famous American trade associations serve highly decentralized economic sectors. Examples include the National Association of Real Estate Boards, the National Association of Retail Druggists, and the American Medical Association.

But life in industrial society is not administered only by trade associations. There are at least three categories of groups, which while not, strictly speaking, trade associations, perform most of the functions of a trade association: the peak association, the organization of agricultural commodities, and the trade union.

The peak association is a group formed primarily by other groups and associations which join together in order to cooperate on a front larger than an individual trade or sector, yet far narrower than a whole class. Robert Brady reports on the same phenomenon in many countries, in particular the *Spitzenverbande* in Germany.[3] Probably the best-known European example was the pre-Vichy French *Confédération Générale de la Production Française*. In the United States the National Association of Manufacturers (NAM) is probably the best-known example; the Amer-

---

[3] Robert A. Brady, *Business as a System of Power* (New York: Columbia University Press, 1943).

ican Farm Bureau Federation (AFBF) is another. Each has a large staff in Washington, the NAM has still another large staff in New York, and the AFBF has an impressive staff in every agricultural state in the country. Their research and educational services are impressive. The AFBF offers various types of insurance along with its other services. The U.S. Chamber of Commerce is another example, with nearly 4,000 local chambers which perform admirably as peak associations for city and regional groups.

Every major commodity in the United States is represented by a commodity organization. These range from immense and aged groups, such as those organized around cotton, tobacco, and wool interests, to very narrow groups, such as one organized by the cranberry growers. Each of these groups is deeply involved in politics, because agriculture is highly politicized. But most of the year's reality for all these commodity groups is administrative. They not only must keep their members informed of the complex price system in agriculture but are deeply involved in the actual implementation of federal and state agriculture programs.

The trade union in the United States was almost self-consciously modeled after business associations. Unions act politically from time to time, and unions do compete in the labor market in a political process called "collective bargaining." But collective bargaining is itself highly bureaucratized, involving elaborate studies of business profits, national economic conditions, prospects for gains outside the wages area (fringe benefits), and problems of jurisdiction. Moreover, most of the year union staffs are busy administering the labor-management contract, not bargaining or campaigning for it. Still other union responsibilities, most particularly job classification, must be bureaucratized if they are to succeed.

The trade association and related groups have gained in importance as factors in the economy of the United States because of the antitrust laws. Certain kinds of direct business cooperation and coordination were considered to be illegal restraints on trade. Trusts were clearly illegal. Pools and market-sharing devices were highly vulnerable to civil and criminal prosecution. Any consolidation that involved a potential competitor was illegal. Private contracts to stabilize markets, even if not illegal, were almost completely unenforceable in the courts. In contrast, the trade association was a structure against which Americans had no particular defenses. Cooperation for advertising, exchange of information, collaborative research, standardization of sizes and grades, and campaigns to discourage cutthroat competition all seemed far enough removed from the problem of excessive economic power or the ideal of the free and unencumbered market. Some associations—for example, the Linseed Crushers' Council and the American Hardwood Manufacturers' Association—have been successfully prosecuted for coercing their members or for helping members conspire to influence prices directly, but as time has passed, the trade associations have become more and more legitimate. This legitimation is the basis for practices of today and begins to suggest why decentralization means delegation of power to these groups.

These are the primary types of interest groups in the country, but they are by no means the only ones. There are multitudes of noneconomic groups—special interest and general interest groups. They are no less oligarchic in internal structure than the economic interest groups. Indeed, this aspect of life is as true of local health and welfare councils as it is of the National Association of Manufacturers. It is as true of the League of Women Voters as it is of the local commerce and industry associations. Groups are run by the few on behalf of the many, and the richer and larger the group the more staff it will have to assume organizational responsibilities. Newer groups, though less bureaucratized, tend to be extremely oligarchic. Many such groups are no more than the leader, a small cadre, and a collection of affiliates of varying degrees of affiliation.

The phenomenon of the formally organized group is a distinguishing mark of modernity—and so, accordingly, is the administration of social relationships. If one defines administration properly—as a relatively formal means of social control through

the use of the most rational possible ordering of means to ends
—it is obvious that modern men prefer administration, for they
are constantly in search of rational controls, in human as well as
physical environments. This must mean increases in routine, in
hierarchy, in oligarchy, in inequality. The phenomenon of the
organized group is also a mark of what social scientists call the
"pluralist system," another mark of modernity. It is true that
groups introduce an important element of competition into large-
scale society. They can interact with one another in a manner that
increases the dynamics of such a society. However, it is romanti-
cism to pretend that life inside established groups is egalitarian,
flexible—in a word, democratic

Decentralization for What?
Groups and the Problem of Governing

Parallel to the development of formal groups is the increased
recognition of such groups as legitimate units of representation.
As syndicalism and corporatism were making their mark in Europe,
so pluralism, interest representation, and more contemporary
variants were gaining ground in the United States. Beginning in the
nineteenth century, precedents were established by government
cooperation with trade associations and commodity associations.
Formal cooperation spread to other types of groups and became
increasingly more systematic as more interest groups established
themselves on a national scale. The Department of Commerce
considered trade associations indispensable in the collection of
business statistics. Agencies in the Department of Agriculture had
been working for a long time directly with a rather large number of
commodity associations and the local farm bureaus of the young
Chamber of Commerce.

Eventually it actually became government policy to encourage groups in areas where no such groups had previously existed. Thus, the Departments of Commerce and Agriculture were instrumental in the formation of, respectively, the Chamber of Commerce and the American Farm Bureau Federation. Various employer and employee associations were encouraged and brought into the internal processes of government as a fundamental part of war mobilization after 1914. But the peak of business and nonbusiness group participation in government came not during war or during reactionary Republican administrations but during the height of the Roosevelt administration. The essential instrument of New Deal industrial planning was the National Industrial Recovery Act of 1933 and its administrative apparatus, the National Recovery Administration (NRA). In good corporativist fashion, the NRA worked through the officially recognized trade organizations. Each sector and service industry and agricultural commodity organized into governing committees of trade association representatives. These representatives developed elaborate codes of fair competition—dealing with prices, wages, exchanges, health conditions, and so on—and, once approved, these codes became federal law.

The NRA was eventually declared unconstitutional as an excessive delegation of law-making power to private groups and government agencies. However, the practice of government controls in cooperation with trade associations did not end; it simply became somewhat less formal and explicit. At present, the Federal Trade Commission could not carry on its business without the regular cooperation of the trade associations and other interest groups. To achieve any regulation at all in the railroad industry, the Interstate Commerce Commission depends almost totally on the associations of railroads for information and administrative services. Almost the same pattern of government-supported self-government by trade association is true in the more ancient trade of shipping and the more recently developed airline industry. The vital role of the commodity associations in the administration of agricultural policy has been identified. In other fields, such as coal mining, insurance, the export trade, space industries, and defense research and development, the official role of trade associations is somewhat more difficult to assess, but their importance in each of these fields is undoubtedly the same.

This official and semiofficial role of the well-organized groups in government during the past half-century merely proves their legitimacy. Their actual scope and significance in American life are far greater. The stamp of governmental legitimacy has blinded the American citizen to the real extent to which his life is being controlled irresponsibly. To anyone with any juridical concerns at all, the trade association represents a dilemma, because it is an exercise in control against which there is no regular defense governed by law. This is also true of the trade union. In more subtle forms it is also true of many noneconomic groups. When a person with an LL.B. degree is denied membership in a state bar association on the grounds that he refuses to reveal his political activities, he has no recourse as a citizen though the denial results in a severe deprivation. When a person with an M.D. degree is denied membership in a state medical society solely on the grounds that he is black, he too has no recourse in the courts. When a minority member of a trade union seeks to organize a competing union in the shop, he is very likely to run afoul of prohibitions against such a thing in legislation enacted and supported even by liberals.

Owing to some colossal misunderstanding or misplacement of liberal sympathies, the most poetic and sympathetic defenses of groups and their official and semiofficial prerogatives of access have come from liberals whose concerns are otherwise for equality and justice. Treating groups as mere interest groups—and disregarding the degree of internal and administrative control of the members—political scientists tend to elevate such associations to an essentially democratic form. When the economist and philosopher-prince John Kenneth Galbraith created the economic model called "countervailing power," he elevated the trade association to a general principle of virtue so precious that he could propose that "support of countervailing power has become in modern times a major peacetime function of the Federal government."[4]

These considerations have a direct bearing on any realistic evaluation of the drive for decentralization. If one sincerely wishes to implement such a goal, one is faced with two possibilities—and two only. One possibility for decentralization is the absence of government altogether, in the spirit of laissez faire. But in our day and age—and this is especially true of the very ones who cry for decentralization—this solution is not acceptable, for it appears to mean abdication to all sorts of forces already considered evil. The only other possible way of implementing the notions of decentralization is to use direct and positive government involvement on the basis of delegation of power. This is undoubtedly what most of the decentralization campaigners have in mind. But delegation of power leads precisely to the kind of group domination and oligarchic pattern of control just described.

When a government program is deliberately and carefully decentralized, it begins with a grant of power and responsibility to an administrative agency. This is called "enabling legislation." Such enabling legislation leads to a decentralization through "delegation of power." The delegating authority—Congress at the national level—must carefully avoid accompanying that delegation of power with any clear standards of guidance in law. If such clear standards were present in the law, Congress in effect would be giving with one hand what it takes with the other, which would not be considered sincere decentralization. This obtains because clear standards at law limit the discretion of the administrator, and the ultimate choices that guide conduct would then be left with the decisions made by congressional authority and the presidential authorities at the center.

Decentralization through delegation of power is the very jurisprudence of the modern liberal state: Give the agency and its

---

[4] John Kenneth Galbraith, *American Capitalism: The Concept of Countervailing Power* (Boston: Houghton Mifflin, 1952).

agents sufficient discretion by keeping the rules of law broad and permissive so that agencies can enter into a true policy-making relationship with their clienteles. True decentralization would then be consonant with liberal belief in the pluralistic process of bargaining. This is the process of decentralization as it is widely described in the professional literature and as it is understood by the campaigners for real decentralization. The traditional notion of rule of law has in effect been replaced by a rule of bargaining. And the rule of bargaining is in turn justified in the name of representation, decentralization, and participatory democracy.

But can we ennoble such practices by calling them true representation or effective participatory democracy, or by applying to them any of the other halo-laden words in the democratic lexicon? When the law passed and promulgated at the center sets no central directions, all the advantages in eventual implementation rest with those elements of the community that are best organized and most sensitive to what is going on. This in turn obviously means the trade associations and all their organized cousins. Sometimes a government program sets out deliberately to create new groups in order to equalize the access a bit. This was done in the war on poverty, and many years before then with the Chamber of Commerce and the American Farm Bureau Federation. In any of these cases the effort to create the new groups to improve countervailing power affects the political situation mainly on the first round of organization, if at all. That is to say, once new groups have been formed, they take on all the oligarchic trappings of previously organized groups, and the character of true representation in the society has hardly been affected at all.

Thus, decentralization through delegation of power to lower levels almost always results in unequal access and group domination of the public situation. However, the situation is far worse when these arrangements for access are formalized as has been the case in the cases of the war on poverty and COMSAT, or in agricultural policy-making vis-à-vis the commodity organizations. It is incredible that this pattern of policy-making could ever be supported by any person sincerely espousing the values of true representation and true political equality. Formal recognition of groups and their representatives for purposes of such participatory democracy converts each group so honored into an official component of government. Such recognition converts what is already an oligarchic situation into an involuntary situation. One of the saving characteristics of oligarchy in groups is that a person may have alternative group memberships and therefore may choose among them. This ability to choose may even give him a kind of consumer influence over the activities and policies of each of the groups. But when groups are officially recognized for purposes of being included in the interior processes of policy-making, the virtues of multiple membership pass out of existence.

Thus, public recognition of a private group gives that group an involuntary character and increases the degree to which persons are subject to hierarchy, without, even at that price, increasing the sum total of real representation. Whether the recognition is formal or merely de facto, social control by irresponsible processes is the result. The notion of the voluntary association becomes more and more an absurdity. On the South Side of Chicago there is a group called the Blackstone Rangers. The group is feared by many because it forces teenagers to be members. However, the difference between the Blackstone Rangers and some other local groups participating in the war on poverty or some educational program becomes less and less easy to discern as that group becomes more and more the officially recognized channel of access to public policy-making. The Blackstone Ranger organizer may say, "Join our organization or I will beat your head in." The community organizer will say, "Join our organization or you will have very little say in community policy-making."

Increasing demands for decentralization are a reflection of increasing distrust of public programs. But direct response to these pleas through apparent decentralization—by further spreading the pattern of devolving programs on organized interest groups—is a complete misunderstanding of the natures of the demand and problem. Further decentralization at the federal level at a time when so much power has already devolved on private structures is an almost certain way of perpetuating the very crisis decentralization is supposed to cure.

It seems that the real question was never one of centralization versus decentralization. Decentralization was always a question of to whom and for what. Decentralization through delegation of power merely meant conversion from government control to a far more irresponsible, enigmatic, unpredictable group control. The only apparent way out of the present crisis is not to yield directly to private claims but quite independently to determine the clear injustices and inequities that are involved and to exercise control over them through clear laws that do not depend on the good wishes or the participatory practices of any of the subjects of these laws. If such laws were for a time properly and vigorously administered by duly constituted governmental administrative bodies— and this has not happened for many years—one might at some point thereafter anticipate a proper and effective decentralization. Until such time as true federal power and a clear national commitment to racial equality and economic equity have been established beyond doubt, decentralization is abdication.

4

President and Congress: War and Civil Liberties

The credibility gap is a new name for an old affliction. It is an affliction of the process of communication between a people and its government. And it is an affliction to which foreign policy in a democracy is particularly susceptible. During the Vietnam War the affliction has achieved epidemic proportions. For many thousands of Americans, opposition to the war is based more on what was said than on what was done.

There may be no way for mass democracies to avoid this sort of affliction. Secret diplomacy is extremely unstable and problematic, and there is still yearning for "open agreements openly arrived at." Machiavelli to the contrary notwithstanding, lying is the greatest risk of all. Appearances may be deceiving at first; but in a free country the lies of the past have a way of being found out and creating the credibility gaps of the future. By spreading suspicion, small lies, once discovered, have a horrible tendency to corrupt larger truths. On the other hand, overcommunication can be as risky as lying. One of the characteristic features of American foreign policy conduct since World War II has been oversell not overkill. It is a variant of Potter's gamesmanship: how to deceive without actually lying. President Truman did not lie when he promoted the United Nations and Marshall Plan. He oversold. He oversold the threat of communism and World War III, and he oversold United Nations membership and the Marshall Plan as remedies. President Johnson oversold the threat of North Vietnam (and China) to our world interests; he then oversold each successive expansion of our military involvement.[1]

Congress reacts angrily to credibility gaps, especially to the widening of the gap through oversell. The 1970 controversy over presidential and congressional war powers is far from unprecedented. Almost exactly twenty years earlier Congress put its prerogatives on the line with almost exactly the same kind of assertions. Much of the debate then focused on the Wherry Resolution, which declared that no troops would be stationed in Europe under NATO "pending the adoption of a policy with respect thereto by the Congress."

This kind of controversy is extremely important. It raises fundamental questions that need raising at least once every decade. But more important, it raises questions that may ultimately narrow the credibility gap. We will never get off dead center, we may never close the ceaseless inflationary gap of war in Southeast Asia, unless we eliminate the general distrust that renders every specific step suspect. Because of the widespread distrust in public authority and public officials, America has become a paranoid society. The most sincere, effective steps toward disengagement in Southeast Asia can never be taken so long as thousands of people suspect that such steps are meaningless or mean something different from the official justifications provided for them. Restoring an effective balance between formal powers is one of the most effective means of restoring trust in public authority. And effective means counterpoise; it means confrontation in setting the general contours and standards of foreign policy—in determining real and lasting national interests rather than imagined affronts to international credibility.

Once general trust in public authority is restored, there can be

---

[1] See *The End of Liberalism,* chap. 6.

a restoration of the clear constitutional power of the President to run the foreign ministry of the country. But until this is done within well-established constitutional roles and processes, it is unlikely that it will be done very well or at all. There is a derangement of powers at present, and no amount of assertion of presidential rights and prerogatives will right earlier wrongs, however well founded those assertions may be. History cannot be rewritten, and the past that created distrust cannot be changed. The credibility gap can be reduced, and trust can be restored, only insofar as the people are satisfied that proper constitutional roles and formalities are being carried out, because ultimately these formal means are about the only dependable means of keeping the lying and the overselling to a minimum.

This means a substantial increase in congressional participation in foreign affairs. This increase is desirable for all the previously stated reasons, and it was desirable even before a pro-Congress position served the goal of deescalation in Vietnam. Congress's role must be defined with extreme care. It cannot be done in such a way as to merely serve immediate interests in bringing the Vietnam crisis to an end. It must in fact begin with the full recognition that the presidency is our repository of war and diplomatic powers and that no one or bundle of acts and resolutions is going to alter that fact. Nonetheless, there is an important role for Congress, and the reduction of the credibility gap and the moving of American foreign policy off dead center is very likely to depend on the proper identification of that role.

A step in this direction would begin by reviewing three interrelated developments that account in large part for the decline of congressional relative to executive power in foreign affairs. From this analysis will also emerge realistic steps toward restoration of Congress in the scheme of separation of powers. (1) Congress has delegated—virtually alienated—much of its power in foreign and domestic matters. (2) Congress has by inaction failed to check a serious and completely unnecessary drainage of its powers and functions. (3) And most important, Congress has failed to seize opportunities for the exercise of powers that are, as a consequence, hardly being performed at all by any agency of government.

Delegation

Ever since the rise of big government, Congress has made a practice of alienating its power. Legalistically, this is called the delegation of power, and it amounts in practice to the enactment of "enabling legislation," which provides almost no guidance for the administrator. But Congress has not only given away its powers; it has done so in the worst possible manner. Rather than attempting to maintain its constitutional role by accompanying the delegations with clear standards and guidelines, Congress has sought instead to create new agencies and maintain old agencies with intimate relationships to congressional committees and independent of the President.

In foreign affairs, the congressional practice of maintaining autonomous agencies produced a veritable cascade of action following World War II. Unification never reduced the autonomy of the separate military services, and even went so far as to create a new major service. The original arrangement for the Secretary of Defense did not even include an Office of the Secretary. Congress sought to keep the civilian secretaries as weak as possible.

Congress gave us a completely autonomous foreign aid program. The debate, the statute itself, and all of the organic documents implementing the Marshall Plan made its independence of the State Department unmistakably clear. The same is true, only more so, of the Atomic Energy Commission. Here the intention of congressional intimacy was made still more explicit by the creation of the Joint Committee on Atomic Energy. This relationship continues to this day.

There are still other examples of this kind of subpresidential delegation. But they all add up to the same pattern. Congressional action has in a sense put foreign policy and war-making powers in a no-man's-land, a Jacob's ladder cut off at the bottom and at the top. While retaining the power to deal on a piecemeal basis with individual agency activity, Congress has at the same time prevented the development of a unified and systematic foreign affairs capacity.

Little wonder that there should be a "military-industrial complex." But there is also an atom complex, an international trade complex, a commerce complex, an agricultural complex, and so on. These complexes are simply highly stabilized, triangular relationships among a congressional committee, one or more sub-presidential agencies, and some private interests of one sort or another. The real world is defined from within these complexes, and (as we saw in Chapter 2) it becomes extremely difficult to impose a different definition of reality that would tend to break down the internal values within each complex and replace them with values over which none of the complexes have any control.

Once the pattern is defined this way, it is obvious that Congress must eliminate it in order to take on the kind of power it now seeks. But it is extremely important to recognize that if Congress expands its power by eliminating these complexes, the expansion will not come at the expense of presidential power in foreign affairs. Congressional delegation of power to agencies has not commensurately expanded the presidency; in fact it has imposed new responsibilities on the office, for which there are never sufficient resources or authority. Thus, if Congress ever really seriously sought to regain a role in foreign affairs, the power of the President would very likely go up, not down. The losers would be the lower level agencies, particularly in the Defense Department. Congressional determination of the criteria that govern the pursuit of national interest would strengthen the hand of the President vis-à-vis his own generals and bureau chiefs while impressing other countries with the determination of the United States to face them and to utilize its resources.

Drainage

Congressional inaction, of course, is not unrelated to delegation. But sins of omission imply inchoate powers, which could reemerge simply in the using. The most dramatic and concrete example of the derangement between the two branches resulting from inaction is the rise of the *executive agreement*. By now, the executive agreement surely enjoys constitutional status. But acceptance of it came during the 1930s, when Congress was giving away everything and the courts were justifying it. And, the Supreme Court in granting the President the right to make such agreements did not suggest that Congress was obliged to accept them.

A thorough examination of the political and legal implications of the executive agreement has never really taken place. The Bricker Amendment controversy of the early 1950s raised the question, but the social motives of the Bricker proponents tended to discredit bonafide efforts to evaluate the executive agreement power. The Bricker people were worried about the fact that executive agreements have the status of treaties, and treaties can be a source of federal domestic power in addition to the express powers of Article I of the Constitution. If, for instance, the United States had become party to an international agreement affecting civil rights, the internal obligations of the agreement would have enabled the federal government—so it was feared—to legislate on matters for which Congress would otherwise have no constitutional power. The opponents of executive agreements were concerned about states rights, whether their invasion came from a treaty or an executive agreement; they were less concerned about congressional prerogatives and the drainage of congressional power in foreign affairs. Yet, the executive agreement combines the worst features of all the means of conducting diplomacy. It combines the formal and advanced commitment of a treaty with the ambiguous and uncertain status of a diplomatic note.

But the executive agreement is only one manifestation of congressional evasion of its responsibilities to evaluate and guide

America's national interest. The role of Congress, especially the House, has indeed expanded through the increased international financial involvement of the United States. However, the appropriations process was never good for anything but the consideration of incremental issues, and a preoccupation with such issues has only succeeded in further blinding members of Congress to the real issues.

This "appropriations approach," coupled with the above-mentioned preference for agency autonomy, the passive acceptance of executive agreements, and probably a sense of being browbeaten by the executive wrapped in the flag, has prevented any serious parliamentary reexamination of America's posture in the world during the last revolutionary decade or two. As a result, some mighty old doctrines and concepts continue to guide our specific actions, not because we necessarily believe in them, but because they are all we have. For example, we continue to operate in the world, particularly in Southeast Asia, as though communism were a single, monolithic world-wide conspiracy. Within that context we still tend to view every outbreak of violence and every *coup d'état* in the world as interrelated and cumulative and to assess every outcome in terms of whether it is "a loss to the free world." A major argument for our being in Vietnam on an expanded basis, for example, has been not only the so-called domino theory, but also the assumption that the Vietcong are puppets of the North Vietnamese, that the North Vietnamese are puppets of the Chinese, and that the Chinese and the Russians are running the show together, so that if we can just win there "we've got 'em licked all over the world."

One cannot fail but be appalled by the overwhelming power of unexamined premises. It is these premises more than any economic interest, or any contractual or treaty commitments (or even the prior presence of American troops), that push us on into the Asian continent. And we hold onto these premises despite the fact that the notion of communism as monolithic was weakened in Yugoslavia, emaciated in Hungary, and annihilated in China, not to mention its drawing and quartering in Africa and the Third

World, in Czechoslovakia, and Lord knows where else. Although the breach between China and Russia is more profound than any breach we have ever had with our historic allies, at least since the War of 1812, the Congress has never on a full-scale basis examined the possibility that there are many communisms, that nationalism is now a stronger force than communism. In the absence of a full and open reevaluation, even the most sophisticated members of Congress, the executive branch and the press frequently refer indiscriminately to any adversaries in Southeast Asia as the "communists." Body counts refer simply to "2,000 communists." A prisoner is a "communist prisoner," whether he is Laotian, Chinese, or Vietnamese. Do all those yellow men really look alike, or is it our racism? I think it is neither. I think it is the blindness imposed by ancient criteria, learned by rote, as to the character of the enemy and the threat against vital national interests.

This is the result of the inaction that has drained so much power away from Congress. Congress cannot have the power to direct a war. But it can define what war is, what the terms of victory are, and, most important, what the stakes shall be. Instead, Congress has allowed the executive, and especially the military, to define the guiding concepts and define the terms of victory. That way we can never win. Winning is a matter of definition. If in order to justify our presence we magnify at each step the stakes and the terms of the conflict, victory becomes unattainable at each step. When we place each conflict in the general context of world communist conspiracy and then depend on executive agencies, particularly the military, to find ad hoc justifications for particular actions, no limit is set on the character of our burdens. In fact there is an inverse relationship between the scope of the conflict and the scope of the justification: The weaker the adversary the greater the need for justification.

There is no reason in the world why laymen, especially when assembled in Congress, cannot set the parameters of international conflict. War is a specialty, and when the layman replaces the specialist, he has a fool for a client. But the conditions of victory and the character of the world environment are not the exclusive domain of the specialist. In fact the specialist may be the least qualified for these kinds of judgments.

This is particularly true when we are speaking of the specialists in war and violence. De Tocqueville expressed grave concern about this particular problem in 1830. In aristocracies, he observed, there is a natural and accepted ranking in society, of which the military career is merely a reflection. There is little pressure or competition among officers of noble rank, for the social distinction between captain and major is not so very great. But in democratic armies the pressure of competition for a limited number of upper ranks is extreme, for these ranks are the only source of available status. Thus, he concludes, the urge to put a military definition on ambiguous, diplomatic relationships is far more common in democratic countries. His essay, "Why Democratic Nations Are Naturally Desirous of Peace, and the Democratic Armies of War," is an ungenerous and anachronistic statement of the case. However, what citizen today is willing to stake his life on the ability of the military specialist to set properly the very conditions within which he himself is to operate?

Powers Unseized and Unexercised

If Congress represents a nation desirous of peace, Congress is not bound to oppose all war. But Congress is responsible for establishing political guidelines of military action, and in the past twenty or thirty years the reverse has more often been the case. Under conditions of crisis, Congress often seeks to do what it cannot do because it will not do what it must. Congress cannot direct this war or any other war. What it can do, and what it has not done, is to set guidelines for direction and limits on the extent of America's commitment.

Congress's war powers, like the President's, are lodged in the Constitution. As Corwin observed, ". . . the Constitution, considered only for its affirmative grants of power capable of affecting the issue, is an invitation to struggle for the privilege of directing

American foreign policy."[2] And in addition to constitutional powers, there is also ample political support for successful congressional participation.

Congress has the constitutional power, which it has not sought to use, to define the objectives and limits of war. If it has the power to declare war, it also has the power to set the terms of war and the character of victory. In the twentieth century, especially since America's emergence as a world power, declared war has come to mean total war, involving a total commitment of population and industrial capacities and, if necessary, the total annihilation of the enemy. But war, including declared war, is a continuum. To treat it otherwise in our age is to combine medieval religious outlooks with modern technology.

Yet, it is Congress that has tended to be the more militaristic and uncompromising, whereas the executive has tended to recognize that war is a continuum. Once American troops are involved in violence abroad, Congress tends to assume a role of protecting the military and adopting its point of view. Some of our most famous military minds are not and have never been military men.

Once war is recognized as a continuum, powers other than the power to declare war become clear. For example, there is no reason why a declaration of war cannot include a number of limiting clauses. Instead of the Tonkin Resolution, an unconditional, *non*declaration of war, Congress would have been far better off declaring a conditional state of war. The declaration of war, or resolutions passed in pursuit of such a declaration, could have defined the limited objectives, the limited character of victory, and even the conditions for armistice. By operating as though war must be either nonexistent or total, Congress abdicated its role through the Gulf of Tonkin Resolution, until 1970, when the situation had become so intolerable that Congress sought in fact to direct the conclusion of the war rather than to set limits within which the executive and the military could conclude the war. In any case, if a

    [2] Edward S. Corwin, *The President: Office and Powers* (New York: New York University Press, 1957), p. 171.

declaration of war does not mean total war, then the congressional declaration could include a number of "whereases" and "now therefores." A state of war is not a state of being but a state of commitment to a certain amount of violence, the degree and character of which are well within the grasp of a body of laymen in Congress assembled.

Some are concerned that the declaration of war is a poor technique for anything short of the actual intent to engage in total war because a declaration of war automatically reduces domestic civil liberties. There is ample basis for such a concern, but it is only as true as we allow it, through inaction, to be. In fact, the very involvement of domestic civil liberties gives Congress's war powers its potentially strong political base as well as an additional source of constitutional power. Let this be put as bluntly as possible: *Most of Congress's effective war powers derive from domestic powers.*

If total war means total involvement of resources and population, then limited war means limited involvement of resources and population. Congress has the power to limit or expand war and other international involvements by setting limits on the amount of domestic involvement. Such limits are directly effective to the extent that they put resources in the hands of the President and the military. Such actions are also effective in symbolizing to the executive and to the world the degree to which the country intends to be involved.

Two brief examples: In the area of conscription, Congress has turned over virtually total powers to the executive. Manpower requirements and the conditions of recruitment, which should be jealously guarded by a great democratic assembly, are considered means by which Congress serves the military. A second sorry example is the general field of civil liberties, of which conscription is a part, where Congress could guard effectively against the more insidious problems of declared war. True, during our two most important involvements in undefined but real wars—Korea and Vietnam—the right to dissent was in large part maintained. But this was owing far more to solid American traditions and the Supreme Court than to any efforts by the popularly elected branches. On the contrary, what President Truman started in his loyalty program became a route through which Congress virtually tried to define the Korean conflict as an undeclared but total involvement. The House Committee on Un-American Activities is but one of those very important instruments by which Congress has tried internally to treat limited war as though it were total war by defining internal dissent as internationally relevant.[3] During the Vietnam War, Congress went still further by cynically adding to the civil rights law a totally unconstitutional amendment to make it a crime to organize for dissent. This is the first federal sedition law since the John Adams administration.

And yet it is in civil liberties that Congress will find political base sufficient "to struggle for the privilege of directing American foreign policy." As De Tocqueville pointed out, and as twenty years of public opinion polls confirm, there are two systems of opinion in the United States, perhaps in any democracy. One system of opinion is nationalistic. It is based on consensus, and, as regards the outside world, is mobilizable and militaristic. The second system of opinion is domestic and libertarian. It is based more on dissent, is selfish, and in a word, noninternationalist. These two systems of opinion are not produced by two entirely different peoples; nor are they the Dr. Jekyll and Mr. Hyde in each of us. Both are essential parts of any country and any people dedicated to its own freedom. But each operates in different contexts, and each responds to different stimuli.

In our constitutional scheme, it was inevitable that the two systems of opinion would attach themselves to different institutions. One of these systems of opinion is attached to the executive. The other tends to be congressional, though there is little effort by Congress as a body to draw from it.

Tables 4–1 and 4–2 only begin to suggest the profound differences in the two systems of politics. Each table is based on a question asked on virtually every poll taken by the American

---

[3] There was a recent change of name to House Committee on Internal Security. For more on this issue, see Chapter 5.

TABLE 4-1

The President's Relation to His Public—
International Events

		"Do you approve of the way the President is handling his job?"
		YES
June 1950	Before Korean outbreak	37%
July 1950	After U.S. entry	46%
August 1956	Before Israeli, British, French attack on Suez	67%
December 1956	After U.S. opposition to the attack	75%
July 1958	Before Lebanon	52%
August 1958	After U.S. marine landing	58%
May 1960	Before U-2 incident	62%
June 1960	U-2 debacle; collapse of Summit	68%
March 1961	Before Bay of Pigs	73%
April 1961	After Bay of Pigs	83%
October 1962	Eve of Cuba crisis	61%
December 1962	After missile crisis	74%
October 1966	Before tour of Pacific	44%
November 1966	After tour of Pacific	48%
June 1967	Before Glassboro conference	44%
June 1967	After Glassboro conference	52%

SOURCE: Theodore J. Lowi, *The End of Liberalism* (New York: Norton, 1969), chap. 6. By permission of W. W. Norton & Co., Inc. Copyright © 1969 by W. W. Norton & Co., Inc. Based on polls of the American Institute of Public Opinion (AIPO). See Nelson W. Polsby, *Congress and the Presidency* (New York: Prentice-Hall, 1964), p. 26, and Kenneth Waltz, *Foreign Policy and Democratic Politics* (Boston: Little, Brown, 1967), chap. 10.

Institute of Public Opinion concerning how individuals feel *in general* about the way the President is doing his job. The question is asked regularly and is not timed or pitched according to any particular national or international event. That is, it does not seek a referendum on a particular issue but only a very general feeling about the President at a given point in time.

These two tables are the result of the following experimental situation. Each item involves some action or event unambiguously associated with the President and his administration. The polls chosen were taken immediately before each action and as soon after the action as polls were available. Inasmuch as no other event of equal importance occurred during the period in question,

TABLE 4-2

The President's Relation to His Public—
Domestic Events

		"Do you approve of the way the President is handling his job?"
		YES
May 1947	Before veto of Taft-Hartley (6/20/47)	57%
July 1947	After veto	54%
Late January 1952	Before steel seizure (4/9/52)	25%
April 1952	After steel seizure	28%*
July 1957	Before troops to Little Rock (9/25/57)	63%
Late October 1957	After troops to Little Rock	57%
Early April 1962	Before steel price rollback	77%
May 1962	After steel price rollback	73%
September 1962	Before troops to Oxford, Mississippi	67%
October 1962	After troops to Oxford, Mississippi	61%
Late May 1963	Before civil rights message	65%
Late June 1963	After civil rights message	61%†
July 1965	Before Medicare passage	69%
August 1965	After Medicare passage	65%‡
June 1967	After Glassboro, before Detroit	52%
August 1967	After troops to Detroit	39%

SOURCE: AIPO polls.

* This survey was taken very soon after Truman announced his retirement. By June, approval of his job had gone up to 32 percent.

† In August it was still 61 percent.

‡ Note that one month later, in September, approval rate was still the same, 65 percent.

there seemed some basis for attributing at least some of any observed variance to the events themselves. It should also be emphasized that the analysis does not rest on any single before-and-after example, but with the over-all pattern as determined by the repetition of identical before-and-after results.

The results demonstrate that the American public is in fact quite capable of expressing very specific responses within very brief periods of time to important leadership situations. We have what V. O. Key in his posthumous work called "responsible electorate." But it is even more interesting to note the character of that responsibility. On matters of international affairs, an event involving the presidency received consistently strong supportive responses. No matter what the situation was, no matter whether the event was defined as a success or a disaster, the people tended to rally around the President in significant proportions. A generally agreed-on disaster, such as the Bay of Pigs, tended to rally people to the President apparently without regard to their attitude toward the event itself. In fact, that costly adventure seems to have been responsible for helping to bring President Kennedy's support to an almost historic high. But even a less important action, such as President Johnson's 1966 visit with former Premier Ky in the Pacific, bolstered the President's faltering popularity.

The figures in Table 4–2 provide a strong contrast. First, domestic leadership actions do not evoke the same degree of responsiveness. But more important, the direction of the responses is almost opposite of those observed on Table 4–1. In the eight important instances on Table 4–2, there was only one in which support for the President actually increased, and this may have been owing to the fact that the follow-up survey was taken very soon after President Truman announced his retirement plans. (Two months later he enjoyed the approval of 32 percent of the public.) The 1962 event helps best to show how clearly the public seems to discriminate between a domestic action and an international one. In September 1962, immediately before the dispatch of federal troops to the University of Mississippi campus, President Kennedy's handling of the job was approved by 67 percent of the sample. Immediately following the occupation of the campus, President Kennedy's standing dropped noticeably to 61 percent. This was mid-October, which happened to be the eve of the Cuban missile crisis. The results of the first AIPO poll following the missile crisis, in December, reveal that general support of the President had jumped well beyond the status quo ante —the Mississippi crisis—to the very high level of 74 percent approval.

These figures strongly bear out the general impression that there are two systems of politics, one international and one domestic. The former is attached to the presidency because it symbolizes sovereignty and international involvement. The latter is congressional to the extent that Congress, the spirit of faction and party, chooses to involve itself in these matters. The political system involved with international affairs is consistently supportive of the government, and is usually supportive on the basis of a two-thirds and three-fourths consensus. The closer we move to total war the closer we can expect this system to move to total consensus. This would naturally be the case, but consensus is artificially moved still higher through patriotic campaigns, propaganda, and legal suppression of dissent.

The other system is not consistently below majority consensus, but its tendency is always downward. This is an inevitable part of our electoral and local party process; these figures are simply a dramatic representation of the restraint that an active electorate is supposed to put on those who are elected. Congress has an obligation to protect and maintain this system of downward tendencies. But if ever there were a practical and selfish argument for civil liberties, here it is. When at any point it is the opinion of Congress that a war is not a total war, it is the time to express this opinion by expansion rather than contraction of civil liberties. Here is a basis of power as well as a fundamental obligation. Joseph McCarthy, HUAC, and many others have proven clearly enough that it is easy to mobilize public opinion against unpopular dissent, especially when the dissent is connected with international issues. But a full analysis of Congress's constitutional power should show that any limitation on dissent eats up Congress's own political base. Total war is, of course, the exceptional case of no public opinion and total executive powers. But how often is there total war?

After Vietnam

It is never sufficient, especially in matters regarding a large democratic assembly, merely to state desirable goals and available powers. Time and again throughout our history we have discovered that good habits must be institutionalized. Congress will never use its constitutional and political powers in an effective foreign policy manner unless it develops a routine and a habit for their use. Thus, what we need is an equivalent in foreign policy to the "automatic stabilizers" built into our domestic economic policy: the Employment Act of 1946, the welfare system, the graduated income tax, monetary powers, and general countercyclical compensatory policy.

The automatic stabilizer in the foreign policy field would have to begin with an organic statute which would require an annual assessment of the state of the world. Pure rhetoric could be avoided by specifying precisely the matters to be covered by the President and by setting up a joint committee, much like the Joint Economic Committee, through which professional papers and regular teach-ins could provide frequent, frank, and unashamed reassessments of such outmoded dichotomies as communism versus the free world.

Congress could require a state of the world report that would go beyond rhetoric. It would include assessments of the state of nationalism in the world and the relation between nationalism and such internationalisms as communism, capitalism, and zionism. Congress could also require that such a report include a review of the status of dissent in this country. Such legislation would require regular evaluation of all laws and practices pertaining to and affecting speech and assembly. It would be ideal if such assessments would lead to regular congressional resolutions regarding the status of the individual in the Cold War. Some of the matters might be quite rhetorical, but the habit of self-evaluation would be most healthy, and appropriate rhetoric often does limit future conduct. Such habits would work as though Congress had temporary injunctive powers against the President, suspending and exposing certain practices until the President has fulfilled some kind of "show cause" requirements. The advantage would be that such injunctions would occur regularly and not merely when crisis renders the power impossible to use. Such a process could also be compared to the budgetary process. It would be elaborate, and it would be a year-round endeavor to review the relation between present effort, present resources, and upcoming stress.

Automatic stabilizers could also be built into international economic activity. A profoundly important stabilizer could, for example, be built by statute into American business through the internationalization of large American corporations. Vastly increased foreign holdings of shares in American corporations would inevitably contribute to world political stability. The United States has been no more eager than the Soviet Union or China to cooperate with international political bodies, owing to fear of the loss of sovereignty. But internationalizing our corporations involves no loss of sovereignty while it is increasing the potential for world stability by increasing actual interdependence and by increasing the credibility of our own commitments to world peace.

Congress also could with very little trouble ease the application of antitrust laws against mergers involving a foreign corporation and a domestic corporation. Hitherto, the Department of Justice has applied these laws with far greater strictness to these than to totally domestic mergers. Congress could also very easily work out programs to encourage more foreign buying of American stock. Precautions against control in certain sensitive industries could easily be written into the statutes.

The purpose of all this, however it might technically be done, would be to introduce the kind of monetary interdependence that was fairly obviously the foundation of what Polanyi has called "the hundred years of peace" of 1814–1914. Countries are far more likely to enter into substantial agreements and to live conscientiously by the terms of those agreements if each country has a substantial stake in the other country. As Polanyi has suggested, the houses of Morgan and Rothschild had more to do with the hundred years of peace than the combined influence of the European armies and the British navy.[4]

There are other automatic stabilizers that a well-motivated imagination could conjure up. Their enactment is Congress's power and obligation. And they should be contrived for the future and not designed for the particular crisis at hand. And their desirability should be obvious to anyone who appreciates the extent to which the whole of the American constitution is built on the principle of automatic stabilizers. Separation of powers, check and balances, federalism, bicameralism are the most formal of the stabilizers built into the system as faith that better government has a better chance when it is the outcome of confrontation.

Confrontation between the executive and Congress is both natural and desirable, in foreign as well as domestic policy-making. One source of serious error after World War II was bipartisanship, largely because it shackled Congress in its relations with the President. Bipartisanship declared open confrontation off limits; this contributed to the direct delegation of power to the lower level agencies and nonpolitical bureaucrats without adding power or legitimacy to either the President or Congress. A careful study of the history of bipartisanship would tend strongly toward the conclusion that confrontation is better than cooperation between President and Congress. Such a review would also support the proposition that an independent Congress boldly exercising its war and peace powers is far more dependable and effective than the party system in governing America's international conduct. Parties, as suggested by bipartisanship, are not dependable in the foreign

[4] Karl Polanyi, *The Great Transformation* (Boston: Beacon Press, 1957).

policy area. No better instance of this can be found than the present situation regarding the Vietnam War. Each pot has called the other kettle black, and they are both correct. Parties are good to a limited extent in inflicting "electoral punishment," to use Kenneth Waltz's felicitous term, on the international policies of the party in power.[5] But this method is not regular and dependable. More important, it is not a constitutional process, and therefore in addition to being undependable and ineffective it also grants little legitimacy to antiwar dissent until the war drags on long enough to make attacks on it a matter of political advantage. When those who made the war later attempt to assume a dovish leadership in opposition, they are simply not very plausible. A more independent Congress might have encouraged some of these people to resign and take their case to the public at a time when their opposition might have meant something. To wait for their party to leave office to say they were the original peaceniks is neither appropriate nor effective.

As a political institution Congress is, of course, capable of the same kind of opportunism. But it is also true that Congress has always been more noninterventionist than the President. If somehow that kind of spirit can be turned into a mature and subtle restraint rather than a kind of flipflop between isolationism and jingoism, we would ultimately develop the kind of responsible American foreign ministry that the world waits for.

It has been said that the military fights current wars with the strategies of each previous war. Congress's obligation is to fight current wars with the concerns of the next. Otherwise, there will be no system within which to realize the hopes for which wars are supposedly fought.

This is what the present constitutional debate is, or should be, all about. Long periods of preparedness—which in our day we call "cold war," "limited war," "police action," and so on—are a serious threat to democracy. Preparedness means mobilization, and

---

[5] Kenneth N. Waltz, *Foreign Policy and Democratic Politics* (Boston: Little, Brown, 1967), chap. 10.

mobilization means limitation of personal freedom. At some point in a long period of preparedness, a people can lose the habit of freedom. And this spells out the dual obligation of Congress in foreign policy. Congress must seek, and has the power to seek, to protect democracy from cold war. And Congress must simultaneously seek to use democracy to set directions and limits on our preparedness. When these two obligations, and their concomitant power, are used to reinforce each other, Congress is obviously performing in a way ideally suited for a mature democratic participation in world affairs.

5

Postwar Panic and the Chilling of Dissent

If involvement in foreign affairs poses basic dilemmas for democracies, the assembly is the one institution most likely to suffer. The power of the assembly depends on the fullest exercise of civil liberties. Yet Congress has had a particularly bad effect on civil liberties since the beginning of the age of preparedness. Though not alone in this among all the government agencies, Congress, through some of its statutes and its committees, has in fact had a chilling effect on its own constituency.

If this is true only in small part, it is almost tantamount to legislative suicide. Has it been true—and, if so, to what extent? And why?

War versus Postwar: Fear versus Anxiety

In American history postwar periods often seem to find the country in some kind of domestic political crisis. The Ku Klux Klan and widespread repression followed the Civil War. The Klan was revived after World War I, and there were other official and un-

A portion of this chapter had originally appeared in "Prognosis for Crackdown: The Wheel of Panic," *The Nation*, May 19, 1969.

official acts of political suppression too well known to require review.

After World War II there was an even more intense panic, during which we developed our notions of encirclement from without and subversion from within. Hardly had the sense of panic begun to weaken when Korea and its aftermath revived it. (Remember that during the late 1940s it had been even difficult to get military budget increases.) The post-Korea panic, while brief, was intense.

Military victory seems to give Americans very little sense of safety. During the war period itself there is, of course, a great reduction of personal freedom. Constitutional safeguards weaken. Dissent is squelched. "Loose talk sinks ships," and all that. But the decline of tolerance during wartime is inevitable, especially in an age of total war. What is curious is how slowly tolerance spreads even after open hostilities have ended and the period of total danger has passed. In a democracy, a postwar era is a very special time. This is in part a testimony to our higher moral feelings. After a war we suffer from war hangover.

Postwar repression is not, however, a mere extension of war mentality. It is special. During war, repression is born of fear. Lives are actually at stake. Enemies are real. Loose talk can sink ships. After the war, when real threats disappear, hypothetical threats seem inevitably to take their place.

While the real threats of real war produce *fear,* the imagined threats of cold war produce *anxiety.* This fairly conventional psychological distinction provides a means for understanding some profound problems of our own times.

Fear is a response to an unambiguous threat, such as a declared belligerent, a gang of thieves, a business monopoly. Against such threats modern men use reason and science. Anxiety arises out of a sense of impending doom. It is the response to undefined causes, the undeclared enemy, the unseen dangers. Panic is the collective version of anxiety, as in a Wall Street panic. In confrontation with anxiety and panic modern men seem to have no advantage over primitives. They resort to unreason and superstition.

In panic, the greater the ignorance of cause and effect, the wider is spread the net of probable causation. If a woman in a primitive society was ignorant of the procreative process and yet wished to avoid having a baby, she might in her anxiety run from every forest creature, every tree, every star, as well as every human being. When modern man wants safety and has no analysis but "disorder" and "subversion," he too begins to see danger in every shadow. Disorder itself, despite the fact that it is a natural condition, becomes unlawful. From acts that are known to cause injury—rape, assault, robbery, murder, adulterated goods, unsafe automobiles, industrial waste—we spread the net of causation to include remote acts that are not intrinsically evil and that do not connect in any provable way to a chain of causation, but that might *tend* to connect in the long run to injuries. Then the net spreads to include conspiracies to do injury, where some acts indicate a possible intention on the part of two or more parties to join the causal chain. The net ultimately spreads to conspiracies to advocate joining the causal chain. At this point anyone can find anything a cause of injury to himself or disorder to his community.

This expansion of the net of causation is the route from panic to reaction, and ultimately to the institutionalization of reaction: activation of the agencies of repression. Like the antidemocratic sentiments that guide them, these agencies are always with us. Reaction is the process by which panic strengthens antidemocratic sentiments and the agencies emerge to vocalize it. They incant their mysterious theories of cause and effect, and it is usually too late to avoid repression by the time the vocal minority fully recognizes it.

These agencies of systematic repression exist at three levels: national, state-local, and nongovernmental, or "organizational." The national level includes, of course, FBI operations under the Smith Act and other sedition powers, the most recent being the Civil Rights Act outlawing conspiracies to cross state lines with the intention of causing a riot. The national level also includes the CIA, though domestic operations are officially off limits. There are also the congressional committees in House and Senate. The social and economic functions of the military come into play, as do such agencies as the FCC, the Internal Revenue Service, and the Post Office, whose powers can to a very great extent be converted to "internal security" whenever the need arises.

At the level of state and local government one observes the expansion of police intelligence agencies, vice squads, and the other special units operating under morals legislation, disturbing-the-peace-type legislation, sedition legislation, and so on. One of the least appreciated but most effective examples of repression at this level is the zoning and planning agencies, which use their powers, particularly in the suburbs, to keep out unwanted social elements behind a façade of objectivity. It includes conversion of state militia into state police. And now a new and growing menace is the rise of the local secret police, or "red squad" as it is termed in Chicago. A rather large proportion of the student and black radical leadership, including some of the most vocal, are paid informers or actual undercover agents.

The reactionary role of nongovernmental organizations, though less appreciated, also tends to intensify during panic periods. The most noticeable aspect of this is the role of patriotic groups, "Christian crusades," veterans associations, and the like in whipping up distrust and lobbying for activation of the governmental instruments of repression. But equally insidious is the direct role of groups, because so often the individual has no legal recourse. The closing off of channels to skills and skilled occupations for minorities has given rise to the beautiful but unproductive irony of picketing against the unions rather than management. The refusal, with complete impunity, by state bar associations and other professional societies to grant licenses to practice to politically unsafe persons is a practice not unknown in the past and likely to return in a new period of panic. Universities are now facing the agonizing problem of distinguishing between the antiintellectuals who are out to destroy the university and the political radicals who have as their haven the university or nothing.[1]

Moreover, there is an interactive effect among these levels and

[1] See also Chapter 6.

agencies of repression. Such an interactive effect is especially significant because of the potential for suggesting a relationship between internal and external "enemies." Much more will be done with this connection in a moment, but suffice it to say here that local investigative agencies are unlikely to turn up international spies, yet belief in the connection between domestic and international threats legitimizes all manner of investigation and control, ranging from local police wars against the Black Panthers to tapping the telephones of Martin Luther King and Mohammad Ali. Is this national security? The Black Panthers did not get into collective trouble with the police in Chicago until their movement came to be defined, during the 1968 Vietnam retreat, as political. The conspiracy trial and the conspiracy title of the Civil Rights Act, under which the trial took place, are products of cold war panic. No-knock and summary detention statutes are products of the same anxieties.

But the effect of panic on the individual dissenter is only part of the problem, and may not be the most important part. Potentially the more serious dimension, perhaps because it is so difficult to define and measure, is the spillover effect of investigations and prosecutions of protest on the whole community—on the *climate* of dissent. The Supreme Court, in *Dombrowski* v. *Pfister,* has called this phenomenon "the chilling effect," a dictum formulated as a judicial constraint against the investigation and prosecution of dissenters by state officials.[2]

We approach the 1970s in an especially difficult situation. Already we feel the first chilling breeze of panic anticipating the end of the war in Vietnam. The panic to come can only be worsened by the incomplete revolution in human relations set off more than a decade ago. At this juncture American institutions seem incapable of dealing with either domestic or international confrontation—and the two together have become virtually unbearable. The Vietnam War is coming to be seen as perhaps America's first clearly illegitimate international adventure, and the

[2] 380 U.S. 479 (1964).

revolution in human rights is more devastating than a crisis such as a depression because it casts a pall of illegitimacy over so much of the political apparatus. Because neither the resolution of the war nor of the domestic revolution is likely to satisfy anyone, it would be prudent to expect one of the most serious reactions in American history during the 1970s.

To gauge the future one has only the past. The most recent data for assessing the potential of the "chilling effect" in the coming years must be drawn from the evidence of the aftermath of World War II and the Korean War. Though the evidence does not provide conclusive proof, it establishes a strong presumption, and for an area of activity as supremely sensitive as that of civil liberties, this presumption must be taken as a criterion of public and private conduct.

Some readers will point to differences between the silent generation of the 1950s and the strong and vocal peace and power-to-the-people movements of today. But even such skeptics would be quick to acknowledge the fact that such activists represent no more than 3 to 5 percent of the young, perhaps still fewer of the black young. Though this is a large numerical increase over the activists of the 1950s, it is still a tiny part of the population.

Moreover, no form of repression short of summary imprisonment chills the dissent of true activists. The problem lies with the uncommitted, whose silence allows repression of protest; the problem lies with the mechanisms by which this silence is expanded and maintained. The chilling effect is the process by which the ever-silent majority are converted from a passive to a supportive audience for repression.

The engines of repression are more numerous and efficient than ever. Phone taps and income tax returns were unknown to Mitchell Palmer. And, though contempt action was available before 1969, there were never any better authorizations for its use or more eager users than today. But among all those agencies of government that possess a zeal for protecting the country from unpleasant utterances, the House Un-American Activities Committee has produced the most explicit record. HUAC provides the best available opportunity to attempt some kind of systematic assessment of the chilling effect. Through HUAC's record we can assess Congress's role in particular as well as the relationship in general between government efforts to regulate speech and the general level of tolerance of unpopular speech.

Many things have been written about the epoch of the late 1940s and early 1950s. Some interpretations are quite contradictory. But one thing can probably be said without provoking much disagreement on any side. This is that the force called McCarthyism succeeded in creating a parallelism or conjunction between international and domestic conflicts. McCarthyism succeeded in defining conflicts between the United States and other nations in terms that were meaningful within domestic political blocs, to the extent that for at least a decade the terms "liberal" and "conservative" conveyed consistent meanings without qualifiers, such as "domestic liberal" or "conservative on international affairs." To those who approved of McCarthyism, this meant that Senator McCarthy had succeeded in making Americans alert as to the real meaning of international conflict and that the meaning was not a mere difference of material and political stakes but rather a consistent and cumulative set of events that could be understood only in ideological terms. To those who opposed McCarthyism, his approach meant the denial of the possibility that other nations, including the Soviet Union, could have normal workaday political and economic interests that were antagonistic to our own. But either way, a connection between external events and internal political behavior seemed to have been established, and that is the character of the problem when one considers the question of civil liberties: *Internal dissent became an international problem.*

Such an interconnection meant that what might have been a healthy distrust of expansive Soviet policies could also become the basis for mistrust and disapproval of internal dissent of all sorts. It was during this very period that the astute British analyst of Americans, Sir Denis Brogan, wrote his classic article on "The Illusion of American Omnipotence," in which he observed that Americans as they emerged into world leadership were increasingly to take the view that any setback in international affairs, such as the "loss" of China, could only be owing to treason, treachery, incompetence, malfeasance of office, or some other factor from within the United States itself.[3]

The connection between international conflict and internal dissent was institutionalized by the Senate Permanent Investigations Subcommittee and by the House Un-American Activities Committee. This was particularly the case with the latter, because it was a regular standing committee, it had been around longer, it had a larger staff, it had an enormous list of names of suspected persons and organizations, and it was run by Senator McCarthy's supporters in the Democratic Party, which was the majority party for all but two brief periods after 1945.

The Chilling of Dissent: An Empirical Test

Back in 1948, Harold Lasswell, one of the founders of public opinion analysis after World War I, observed:

During a war or war crisis the inhabitants of a region are overwhelmingly committed to impose certain policies on others. If the outcome of the conflict depends on violence and not debate, there is no public under such conditions. There is a network of sentiment, groups that act as crowds, hence tolerate no dissent.[4]

It seems, however, that during the shaky peace of the early 1950s, national leadership, with the help of these congressional committees, succeeded in creating what William James would call "the moral equivalent of war." For, as the data show, the expressed tolerance of dissent seems to have been greater during

---

[3] "The Illusion of American Omnipotence," Harper's, CCV (December, 1952), p. 21 ff.

[4] Harold D. Lasswell, "Structure and Function of Communication in Society," in Wilbur Schramm, ed., Mass Communication (Urbana: University of Illinois Press, 1949), p. 113.

World War II than during the height of the McCarthy period in
1953 and 1954, a period of peace: *All of the following figures
point in the same direction. During the 1950s there was less willingness to tolerate unpopular opinion than during the early and
mid-1940s, despite the fact that during the 1940s we were fighting
a total war.* (Figure 5–1. a, b, c)

Figure 5–1 is the result of a non-directive question. Respondents
could have had fascism or American racism in mind, or the
Soviet Union as such, just as well as international communism.
They could also have had in mind such nonpolitical ideas as free
love or libertinism, or pornography. Yet, there was a noticeable
difference in positive feeling toward the issue of unregulated, first
amendment rights in 1943 or 1945 on the one hand, and 1953 on
the other.

Now, it is quite probable that many respondents answered ques

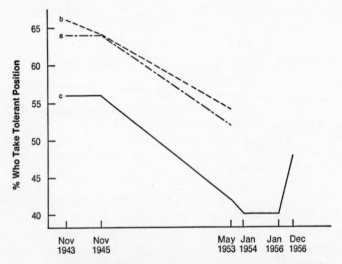

a. "In peacetime, do you think people in this country ought to be allowed to say anything they
want in a public speech?" (— — — — —) (% who said yes)

b. "In peacetime, newspapers should *not* be allowed to criticize our form of government."
(— — — — — —) (% who disagree)

c. "In peacetime, do you think the Socialist party should be allowed to publish newspapers
in this country?" (————————) (% who said yes)

FIGURE 5–1. Public Tolerance of Dissenting Opinions, 1943–1956
SOURCE: *National Opinion Research Center*

tions about civil liberties without intending their approval to apply to the war itself. And after all Americans fight wars to make the peace safe for democracy. But the statistical patterns are not presented in order to show how tolerant Americans are during wartime. The contrast between the war and peace periods shows only how weak is the structure of tolerance, even in relation to war years, whenever a campaign of anxiety mobilization is conducted. The data suggest that Americans are responsive, particularly sensitive, to connections between international and domestic problems—and especially where communism is concerned.

Figure 5–1.b is strongly supportive. Here the question is directed specifically toward the left and toward a well-organized form of expression thereof. However, it must also be kept in mind that there had been socialist parties in the United States for years before World War II, and that one of those parties was led by one of America's most respected dissenters, Norman Thomas. It should also be kept in mind that our closest ally, Great Britain, had, by 1951, been ruled for six years by a socialist party, which had proven how mild and responsible a so-called socialist party can be. In this context, therefore, note that during the darkest moments of the war more than 55 percent of a national sample approved of the publication of a socialist newspaper, whereas a decade later this approval had dropped to below 45 percent and was not to approach a majority again until 1957.

These data must be taken in the still broader context of the epoch in question. By 1953–1954 the Korean War was actually over. One of our great contemporary heroes was in the White House. The "period of maximum danger," as defined by the National Security Council in its famous NSC–68 White Paper of the late 1940s, had passed. NATO was very much a going concern, adding greatly to our sense of security. We had even succeeded in making our peace with our enemies of World War II, a peace very much to our own military advantage. We had made equitable and balanced arrangements with the countries that excited enmities on our right as well as our left. That is to say, we had successfully concluded quite advantageous agreements with such countries as Spain and Yugoslavia, Israel and the Arab states. In 1953 we had even made an adjustment, after four years, to the fact of Soviet possession of atomic capacity. The Marshall Plan had helped produce an economic miracle while helping to prove that the threat of communist takeovers in Italy and France was past.

Why, then, was there a decline in community tolerance of the unpopular at this particular time? The data suggest, without of course proving with complete certainty, that the campaign against the Soviet Union as a "world communist conspiracy" had succeeded all too well, because it had succeeded in defining our antagonisms in such a general and ideological way that they did, in fa૮ ૽, affect First Amendment freedoms and our general political atmosphere far beyond important questions of international relations. With the establishment of the notion of "Fifth Amendment communists" dissent had in effect become heresy.

Obviously, the causal relationships among all of these events are much too complicated to untangle even with far better data than we have. However, the observed patterns do seem to support the proposition that in such periods of social mobilization, dissent seems to be an early casualty. Figure 5-1.c shows that between 1945 and 1953 support for a free press had shrunk to a bare majority of respondents. Perhaps more people could have been mustered to the defense of a particular paper over a particular piece of criticism, but the evidence of Figures 5-1 suggests shrinking confidence that American institutions are healthy enough to withstand criticism without the husbandry of vigilant public bodies.

Figure 5-2 adds two dimensions to the analysis. First, during the years in which the greatest numbers of investigations took place and the greatest stress was put on the connection between external conflict and internal subversion, the members of the community intensified their fears of one another. Second, there seems to have been a split along educational and ethnic lines. Among college people there appears to have been a steady reaffirmation of trust in the community, but there was a noticeable decline of such feelings on the part of the least educated. The

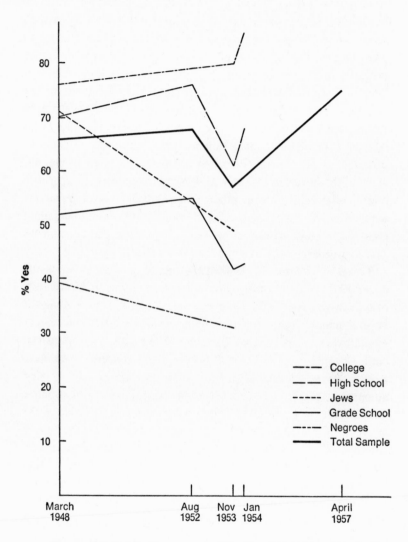

FIGURE 5–2. Public Responses to "Do You Think Most People Can Be Trusted?"

differential impact along ethnic lines is still stronger. Among Jewish respondents, feelings of trust dropped from 71 percent to 57 percent between 1948 and 1953, despite the fact that their median education is a good deal higher than most religious or ethnic groups. Negroes, only 39 percent of whom felt in 1948 that people could be trusted, had shifted even further down the scale by 1954, when only 31 percent expressed feelings of trust. By way of comparison, Stouffer reports that in 1948, when 66 percent of the U.S. national sample felt people could be trusted, only 7 percent of a German national sample expressed similar feelings of trust. We should consider ourselves fortunate in relation to German experience; however, we should remember from that experience that general confidence in others is an indispensable requirement without which countries can have critical difficulties maintaining currency, credit, exchange, political bargaining, parliamentarianism, and general public legitimacy.

These findings for the 1948–1954 period, as well as our tentative explanation for them, can be further reinforced by analyses of the public's responses to the assassination of President Kennedy. Several major studies reported that a majority of the American public expressed belief that Oswald had not acted alone and that "other people were involved."[5] Scholars and concerned organizations attributed this situation to the activities of extremist groups, attempting to revive a " 'conspiratorial' orientation toward public events (that) was undoubtedly quite common during the McCarthy era. . . ."[6]

Yet, despite these feelings of conspiracy, and despite whatever efforts there were to encourage such beliefs, *feelings of distrust toward others in the community did not seem to spread or intensify.* The public had heard charges of communist, Cuban, and even CIA conspiracy. They had witnessed the live television coverage

[5] Reported in Paul Sheatsley and Jacob Feldman, "The Assassination of President Kennedy: A Preliminary Report on Public Reactions and Behavior," *Public Opinion Quarterly,* 28, no. 2 (1964), 211 ff.

[6] *Ibid.,* p. 212. The authors quote Daniel Bell on Freud's observation that "It takes a high degree of sophistication to believe in change; primitive fears are allayed more easily by a devil theory of politics."

of the shooting down of the accused in what could have been interpreted as a daring move by an organized band. There was even awareness of alleged connections between Jack Ruby and organized crime. Yet the relatively high level of trust in others that had been reestablished by 1957 (see the Figure 5–2 trend line for the entire sample) was completely unshaken by the assassination. Between 1957 and November 1963, nearly 75 percent of the general public typically responded affirmatively to the survey proposition, "Most people can be trusted." After the event, the national survey reveals that willingness to trust others had actually increased to 77 percent.[7] Thus, not every type of event, even some of the most poignant, affects public tolerance for the exercise of civil liberties. The assassination, the extended crisis of succession, the year of investigations and hearings ending with the Warren Commission Report, do not seem to be associated with results similar to those of the early 1950s.

Too many things happened in the 1945–1954 period to allow for simple causal explanations of any given phenomenon. This would be true even if the data had been the result of studies more directly designed for this particular task. However, many events and trends of that period could have led me to predict the very opposite of the patterns emerging from in my analysis. For example, a reasonable expectation based on Lasswell's generalization about public opinion in wartime, *supra,* would have been for a general *improvement* in the status of dissent and dissenters after 1945. This expectation is furthered by the puny size and activities of the American Communist Party. According to Bell, Europeans always found the communist issue in the United States quite a puzzle. There was no mass Communist Party in the United States such as the ones found in postwar Italy and France. The Communist Party in the United States, in fact, never had more than 100,000 members, and during the period in question its membership was dwindling rapidly. It had already been thoroughly re-

---

[7] *Ibid.,* p. 213. Their figures also reveal that the assassination had no appreciable effect on the public's willingness to tolerate speeches of communists on the radio, or to encourage racial integration of the public schools.

pudiated by almost the entire American noncommunist left, without any assistance from the governmental commissions or committees. Within four years of the end of the war—prior to the onset of the McCarthy period—communist-controlled unions represented fewer than 5 percent of the labor union membership in the United States. This compares to 20 percent of union membership in 1944–1945.[8] *Thus, at a time when there seemed to be less to fear than ever in the objective situation in the United States, we observe in all the available data the opposite tendency.* Moreover, there seems to be only one pattern that would explain results in public opinion contrary to what one might reasonably have expected: *During the same period there was a palpable increase in federal investigatory activity.*

These parallel patterns are offered in full awareness that statistical association does not constitute causal linkage. The purpose here, as earlier, is to establish a presumption that cannot be denied without overwhelming evidence to the contrary.

Figure 5–3 presents a clear picture. In 1946, the first full year in which HUAC enjoyed status as a regular standing committee of the House of Representatives, a mere three days of hearings on subversive activities were held. One of these days was devoted to hearings on Gerald L. K. Smith, a spokesman of the right wing, and two days were devoted to the activities of left-wing people and organizations. In 1947, a year of reaction following World War II, twenty-eight days were devoted to hearings by HUAC. Each year and each congress thereafter, the days of dedicated activities by HUAC increased until it reached its peak in 1953. After 1954, HUAC's activities went into a continual decline until the low point in its entire history as a standing committee, the eighty-eighth Congress. As racial relations began to fray during the late 1960s, there was some increase in HUAC's activities. There is no indication that the main thrust of its hearings will change—that of making a connection between internal dissent and international

[8] Daniel Bell, *The End of Ideology* (New York: The Free Press, 1960), pp. 100–102.

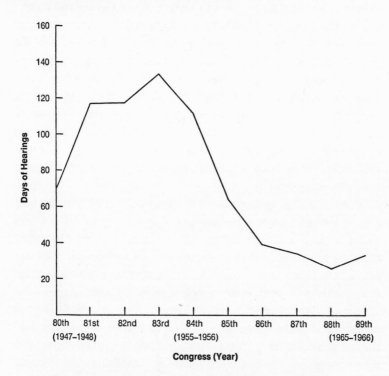

FIGURE 5-3. Days Devoted to Public Hearings, by HUAC

conflict.[9] And there is no reason to believe that the consequences to those immediately concerned are or will be any different. *The difference still lies in the scale of the committee's activities,* which since 1952–1954 simply have not reached proportions and publicity sufficient to influence a national cross-section.

There are no comparable figures on the activities of the Senate Permanent Investigations Subcommittee. However, the only period

[9] For example, the mild-mannered new chairman, Walter Ichord: "It is the committee's hope . . . to keep the American people . . . alert to the fact that communism is a very real problem and danger, both here at home and abroad; that it must be fought here as well as abroad." Or the late Joe Pool on the "tremendous work the Committee has done the past few years in exposing militant pro-Peking Chinese Leftist Communists, who are on the campuses of many of our universities here in America."

in which Senator McCarthy was chairman was during the eighty-third Congress, 1953–1954. McCarthy had been active and had enjoyed regular front-page coverage since 1950, but he had his primary platform only during the period of maximum pressure on public opinion. The reduction in Senate investigations is dated from the culmination of McCarthy's influence, beginning with the Army–McCarthy hearings and ending with the Senate investigations of McCarthy and his ultimate censure by the Senate. *Senate and House activities both declined thereafter* and, *as is noted in Figure 5–2, there is an upsurge of the willingness of individuals to trust one another.*

In sum, official, governmental activity in the civil liberties field can, under some conditions, produce what the Supreme Court has called a "chilling effect." The data tend to support the initial hypothesis that *public tolerance declines in association with the rise of governmental investigations and prosecutions of dissent and that public tolerance returns only slowly as such government actions decline.* Granted, events alone, without any leadership or public investigations, can discourage trust and expand censorship. But it is nonetheless clear that government investigations and prosecutions constitute a clear factor in establishing the connection between certain events and the general level of tolerance. Such mobilization of intolerance is usually one of the express purposes of postwar prosecutors. Thus, if we are to protect civil liberties, we must restrain government regulation of civil liberties, first, because such regulation is so likely to discourage tolerance. Second, we should restrain these investigations and other intrusions because we are able to restrain this kind of intrusion even when the events themselves are not subject to our power. Third, Congress should restrain its own committees because the chilling of dissent quickly shrinks Congress's own power.

Americans have always had faith in the capacity of the democratic process to solve its own problems. Thus far in our history, periods of suppression have been relatively small and temporary. Perhaps. But there is no guarantee that this will always be the case, for the techniques of repression grow with technology, whereas defenses against them do not change appreciably.

No alleged enemy of democracy has the capacity to weaken democracy, certainly not without atomic bombs. But the custodians of democracy do possess such a capacity, through serious misuse of their powers. We thus have no choice but to place the burden of justification on the officials, and the justification must be clear and undoubted, for those who have power possess the weapons of stealth as well as the weapons of might.

PART III

HIGHER EDUCATION: THE ROOTS OF CONSTRUCTIVE ALIENATION

6

Today's Revolution: A Political Analysis of Higher Education

Life is paradoxical. The more responsive the public has been in providing and expanding educational opportunities the more the universities seem to be threatened by hostile forces and instability. It seems that the faster the educator and the education-oriented politician run after their constituencies, the greater the latter's feeling of alienation.

Since World War II the United States has experienced a revolution in higher education. There has been a revolution in facilities, in the scale of demand for higher education, and most clearly in the commitments of governments and educational policy-makers to higher education. The American college population, already large among industrial states, tripled during the last twenty years. During the past decade the expansion was from 3.1 million students to 7 million students; this means that new colleges were opened at the rate of almost one per week. As George Keller in *The Nation* put it, between 1957 and 1967, as much college and university capacity was added to the country's educational resources as had been provided during the previous 300 years.[1]

---

[1] George C. Keller, "The Cost—and Price—of Education," *The Nation,* Vol. 210, No. 8 (March 2, 1970), p. 242.

This chapter first appeared in *PS,* 3, no. 2 (Spring 1970). Copyright © by the American Political Science Association, 1970.

These figures do not account for the revolution in the amount
and variety of higher education being offered outside colleges and
universities. Governments, large industries, trade associations, and
other large institutions offer a variety of courses that would have
standing in any university. What General Motors or the UAW
spend for educating their members clearly exceeds the budget of
many a college in the United States.

So clear has been this relationship between the expansion and
the instability that one is tempted to say that the effort was the
cause. This is a distinct possibility. Our remarkable ability to
provide physical plants, teachers, and quality courses for higher
education is admired and emulated the world over. Despite the
complaints one hears, compared to Europe the quality is high
even as measured by access to professors. The crunch does not
come, therefore, from insufficient response or poor quality, but
from the change in substantive output of the university. That is
to say, higher education in America has been undergoing almost
imperceptibly, but no less clearly, a revolution in the character
of its activities.

This revolution in substance, or output, cannot be attributed to
the demands for more education. Demands on the scale of thousands and millions are simply not that specific. One might get the
impression from critics and from administrators that universities
have been responding to the "educational needs" of capitalism.
But these needs are largely mythical, created not so much by
the business people as by eager college recipients according to
Friedrich's "rule of anticipated reaction." Changes in the nature
and function of the university were made by donors, legislators,
and college administrators. But quite specifically, the primary
influence has been that of educational philosophers and policy-
makers, primarily college presidents and representatives from the
upper regions of the large bureaucratized philanthropies. Surprisingly enough, business executives have not been particularly
influential; for their specific needs, they can and do train their
own people.

During the course of the expansion, educational philosophers

and policy-makers redefined the university in theory and in practice in ways that made the crunch against the established university way of life inevitable. And the crunch would have come
regardless of the unexpected pressures of the Vietnam War and
the race revolution. The crunch has more to do with the inherent
problems of the university than it does with any environmental
factors, however important these factors may be.

The students were first to see that the universities and colleges
were becoming a problem for the members of that community.
They articulated their problems badly, and their analyses were
further confused by the stupidity of many of the reforms they
proposed. Nonetheless, underneath all the childish rhetoric was
an astonishingly appropriate analysis.

Quiet Politicization

The students were first to see, for example, that the functions
around which the universities expanded were biased. They were
the first to see and to articulate the fact that all services rendered
by the university, including the service of producing students as
degree products, involve the university in collective, institutionalized commitments to society. The students were first to perceive
that institutional commitments unavoidably involve the entire
university in directions that seem unmistakably to favor the status
quo. They were the first to see that services in the contemporary
university are essentially policies, that policies involve collective
choices, that collective choices involve advantages and disadvantages in the struggle for rewards that society has to offer, and that
such struggles involve power, which is the very opposite of the
ideal of education.

Little wonder that students are trying to politicize the university. It was clear to them that the university had in its own
quiet way already become politicized. Little wonder that many

radical students demanded the right to use the university as a sanctuary from which they could make their forays into the society. Already the university centers and the service institutes represented exactly that pattern. Little wonder that students demanded participation in university decision-making. Increasingly, universities are making essentially governmental decisions when they perform their services, and when universities act like governments, it is consistent for students to demand the privileges of citizenship.

Finally, it is no wonder that students cry for "decentralization" in the university, despite the fact that the organizational structure of all universities is already overwhelmingly decentralized. (See Chapter 7.) In their own innocent way, students have actually been trying to hold the university to its own pretensions. In so doing they have revealed the nauseating degree to which the universities have prostituted themselves and that this prostitution was not inevitable nor is it unchangeable.

Dynamic Stalemate

But the students are by and large a mere reflection of the revolution and neither a cause of it nor a channel for the ultimate resolution of its problems. One need only examine the demands being made by the student leaders and their faculty fellow travelers to see that their way is not significantly different from that of the Establishment. They have taken their educational models and philosophies from the Establishment philosophers, have generally accepted them, and have simply demanded a new establishment and services to a new set of masters. This is a dynamic stalemate. The sides have agreed on the terms of discourse and disagree on who shall rule. This means that any serious concession involves a change of regime as well as a change of policy. Nothing is more rigid or terrifying than a political situation in which regime and policy are at issue at the same time. Something good could come of it, however, if the alternatives were well enough defined.

Trying their best to get us out of this box, the peacemakers of the university world have posited some comfortable but false alternatives. Most of their discussion takes the form of choices among three functional alternatives. For some of them, the question is between the university that teaches and the university which serves. For others the choice involves a mix among teaching, research, and service. For most peacemakers, the question is simply one of establishing a balance among these functions. The impression is easily gotten that this balance is achieved by each of the corners of this triangle receiving equal emphasis in the life of the university. These are all false alternatives, whether one uses them to make peace or war inside the university.

A proper analysis of the politics of the university must begin with a clarification of the functions of the university, or better, its corporate identity. And the best way to do this is to identify and then discard the definitions of the leading contemporary educational philosophers. The inadequacy of contemporary attempts to define the university can be illustrated by posing a debate between Clark Kerr and Jacques Barzun. There is always some surface validity to the words of Dr. Barzun, and his expressions of concern following the Columbia crisis are a case in point: "I have nothing against the university studying social problems or commenting on what is going on out of its fund of knowledge. But the university is getting to resemble the Red Cross more than a university, with direct help to whoever is suffering." But Dr. Kerr's response is also extremely meaningful: "People who say we should offer no service to society through the modern university overlook that the earlier universities to which they refer provided another, old type of service—to the aristocracy and to some of the élite professions." Dr. Kerr then urged, in a manner that seems at face value quite consistent, that we simply turn from one type of service to another, providing some of the lowest classes with a few more of the highly prized services of the university.

This brief debate between Barzun and Kerr accomplishes a

couple of very important things. First, it illustrates how easily even the most experienced of college administrators fall into the habit of talking about university outputs in the simple terms of service versus teaching and research. But more important still, it underscores the *impossibility of establishing a university that does not have a systematic bias toward one set of social interests and against some other.*

Dr. Barzun falls into the trap of assuming that the university can be free of all services, and Dr. Kerr very correctly points this out. Barzun's whole career represents the case rather well. In his work and in his writings, he represents a liberal arts ethic. This is clearly only one definition of what universities have been or have done in the past 100 years. Moreover, a close look at universities performing such functions will reveal an extremely close affinity between them and the middle classes of 75 years ago or today. Some fifteen years ago Dr. Barzun argued that his kind of educated man would happily pay for admission to Yankee stadium just to talk to others like himself. This is a marvelous image of the type and character of education Dr. Barzun has in mind. But one certainly cannot say that such an output is neutral. It is not a service in any contractual sense, but it is certainly a service in the sense of functional interdependence.

Properly described, the liberal arts college has a consumer ethic. The notion of education in such an institution is a form of dilettantism; this is an admirable notion for those who wish it and can afford it, but it does not satisfy the mass of explebes who constitute the overwhelming majority of students today.

Universities and Social Interests

Fortunately, Dr. Barzun's notion of a university is only one of several possibilities, and more fortunately still, Dr. Kerr's opinion does not represent the only alternative to Dr. Barzun's. Table 6–1 may help to put the issues in a new and productive context. It shows how limited is the Barzun ideal; but it will also show the Kerr alternative to be complete sophistry and rationalization. It shows, for example, that the notion of service that Kerr has in mind is not at all the same thing as the kind of service implied in the liberal arts tradition. It will also show quite clearly that the Kerr definition is intimately shared by the large business and government technocracies and the new left militants.

Table 6–1 is simply a list of primary university functions, the type of man who would be oriented toward each type of university, and the particular social interest that is most consonant with each system. This is not to suggest that the social interest in question determined or in any other way "caused" each educational system. The relationship is rather one between a service provider and a service demander, or between an agency and a clientele. A university will take root and prosper if it has a social base, and it will wither away and disappear if it does not.

The British civil service offers a dramatic representation of the connection between an educational system and dominant social interests. During the 1850s Lord Macaulay instituted a rudimentary merit system in order to modernize the service and eliminate patronage. In 1870, fifteen years after its establishment, the Civil Service Commission had succeeded in imposing competitive examinations as the normal mode of entry. However, this brought about very little change in class composition among higher civil servants because the examination reflected the type of education that one could only acquire at Oxford or Cambridge, which was indeed higher education in Britain. Many years passed before the symbiotic relationship between education and the upper classes was altered.

In the United States a similar pattern is discernible, though not so clearly, because dominance by one or two schools is not so clear and social class stratification not so well established as in Britain. Nonetheless, it is no coincidence that exclusive preparatory schools such as St. Paul's, St. Mark's, and Groton emerged with an upper class of some size and national standing. And,

TABLE 6-1

Educational Systems and Class Interests

Educational Norm	Educational Ethic	Social Interest Represented
Classic education [classic church education]	Consumer ethic Knowledge for its own sake [Knowledge for personal discipline]	Aristocracy
Liberal arts education	Consumer ethic Renaissance man genteel erudition	Old bourgeoisie
Disciplinary education	Producer ethic the Ph.D. the major	New middle classes: Professionals Salariat
Practical education	Training ethic* A & M experience	Working classes
Technocratic education	Problem-solving ethic the multiversity service	Regimes

* Deemphasized during the nineteenth century and now being reactivated through the community college movement, many black studies courses, and the romantic commitments of the young left.

though attacked as early as 1830, the Greek and Latin admission requirements persisted in the East for many years, along with the practice of classifying students by year of entry, putting them up for degrees year by year without any measure of achievement except perhaps in social graces. Harvard, Yale, and Princeton, as well as most of the colleges in the West and South that the latter two helped found, held quite officially to the orthodox view. Only Virginia was experimenting before the midcentury, and it is significant that the Democrat Jefferson organized his college not according to the principle of the practical arts but according to rudimentary disciplines: ancient languages, modern languages, mathematics, natural philosophy, natural history, anatomy and medicine, moral philosophy, and law. This anticipated by many years the pattern that was ultimately to become dominant in America. But until that time, classical education, reinforced and guided in the United States by the Biblical and sacred basis of education, was dominant. And its support by and in the established upper classes is unmistakably clear.

As the colleges of the late nineteenth century began to expand, they seemed to throw off two important tendencies—or at least to deemphasize them. Looking at this effort reveals most clearly the relationship between any educational output and important class interests. One of the tendencies was the classical norm, which made no sense to the new universities, such as Cornell and Michigan, founded and expanded on the basis of a new egalitarian spirit. During this period classical and theological emphases began to be toned down at Harvard, and after a bitter battle Yale followed suit. Also deemphasized was the principle of practical education that had begun to take root in the new university but seemed to get nowhere. Despite all the incentives provided by the Morrill Act of 1862, schools based on this principle felt, according to Handlin, "the pressure to change their purposes almost as soon as they opened. Their students did not aspire to careers as farmers or mechanics; nor were the faculties content to teach the skills of field or shop."[2] Thus, any turn toward the practical arts or higher education for the working classes was clearly premature.

Colleges did not become uniform during the late nineteenth century, but there does seem to have been uniform emphasis among their various efforts at reform. These efforts were probably signaled by the election of Charles W. Eliot to the presidency of Harvard in 1869 and his attempt to deemphasize the classical

---

[2] Oscar Handlin, *America—A History* (New York: Holt, Rinehart & Winston, 1968), p. 597.

curriculum. Eliot was one of many reformers, but science was the primary instrument and thrust of his as well as other efforts. Science and scientism pulled university emphasis together from both ends—the classical extreme and the practical extreme— toward an undefined center. As Harvard challenged its own orthodoxies, Illinois Industrial University became The University of Illinois, the proposed A & M of Ohio became Ohio State, and enrollment in agriculture courses at Vermont and Wisconsin vanished. In 1873, Cornell, only in its fourth year of operation, was simultaneously attacked for debasing classical studies and investigated for neglecting agricultural and mechanical studies.

Despite many variations, the middle to which the colleges were being drawn was represented by Andrew Dickson White, cofounder and first president of Cornell University. This was the ideal of the university that would serve scholarship in a spirit of free and universal inquiry, and one in which all studies would be equal as well as equally available. To go along with White's ideal, there developed an entirely new institutional type. This institutional type emerged first at Johns Hopkins (1886), Clark (1889), and in fullest bloom at the University of Chicago (1892). But the principle of equality among organized and institutionalized subjects quickly became a prevailing emphasis at such places as Cornell and Michigan, then slowly but surely at Harvard and Yale, and ultimately at virtually every state university and private university in the land. This was a commitment to an American variation of the German university. It meant the Ph.D., and it meant the marrying of the practical to the theoretical with a never-ending emphasis on the "spirit of inquiry." It meant quite clearly a fusion of teaching and research, a fusion that has resisted all efforts by such people as Clark Kerr to crack it. It was on the ground of this German or disciplinary or scientific norm that the aristocrat-reformer Eliot of Harvard could meet the democratic, radical Angell of Michigan.[3]

[3] See Lawrence R. Veysey, *The Emergence of the American University* (Chicago: University of Chicago Press, 1965), esp. chap. 2.

Discipline and Department

These new principles were institutionalized in the academic discipline, and the prevailing principle of university organization became the department.

From the few basic departments anticipated by Jefferson, the pattern proliferated until it reached the proportion of the early University of Chicago. Political Economy split into Economics, Political Science, and Sociology. (Anthropology was a later split.) Languages were subdivided into separate departments. Biology, once established as a discipline, broke down into many departments. At the graduate and professorial levels the department became a way of life. Each discipline became professionalized. For each, a national society developed, and this became a primary means of diffusing knowledge as well as creating a market and a uniform standard of reward for professors and professorial output. In a sense this was an organizational effort to approximate the truth. It was an effort to represent in the most concrete form the idea that knowledge was a producible and organizable commodity. There is little question that the entire posture of this kind of education, this attitude toward learning and knowing, is characteristic of a very distinctive class.

Another central tendency between the extremes of the classical and the practical was the liberal arts. Though strong in its own right, it tended to maintain itself as a reaction to scientism and the departmentalization of knowledge. Perhaps it was inevitable that the most grandiose effort at real organizational revolt against departments and professionalized knowledge came in the college at Chicago where Robert M. Hutchins, with his great books and his faith that knowledge is unified and timeless, presided over the university that had helped adapt German principles to American education.

The Hutchins experiment did not outlast the Hutchins presidency, nor was it widely copied despite being universally studied. Basically this was because it was, for all his good intentions, a throwback to the pattern of schools-in-service to higher classes. The liberal arts student possesses a consumer ethic, an orientation toward genteel erudition that did not have wide appeal among the newly professionalizing classes, and especially among those who aspired to something less than, or had too little talent for, universality. The liberal arts reaction also failed to dominate because it could be so easily accommodated to the disciplinary principle of organization. The disciplines can coexist with classical and liberal arts orientation by departmentalization. The refinements can continue to exist admirably as "majors." But not so the other way around. To the classicist or the humanist, Plato cannot be departmentalized. The disciplinary system, seated in departments, could, therefore, on the one hand accommodate the notions of science and producible and organized knowledge and on the other hand live easily enough with other approaches to learning and other principles of knowing. Other classes, powerful but small, could be accommodated without any longer having their own universities.

Technocratic Service

It is only when one gets to the newer, technocratic system of education that one finds novel notions of service and alien principles of organization. Clearly, the first three educational norms perform services only in the sense that they are in basic consonance with certain class interests. This is service in a sociological or functional sense and implies merely that there is a section of society in which a certain kind of educational output can find a home. In contrast, the technocratic system means service in an institutional and deliberate sense. It means service as a matter of conscious policy, as in a master-servant relationship. Service in this sense is clearly not the same as in the other, and yet thousands of college administrators and faculty, like Kerr, continually refer in a pseudosophisticated manner to university activism and commitment as though all services have the same significance.

As a matter of sheer survival universities and colleges have always performed some of these master-servant type services. But traditionally these were feared and usually were kept within separate centers attached to the general institution or in centers housed in separate institutes, such as extension services within agriculture schools otherwise run along departmental lines. Or, these services have been contracted on an individual rather than an institutional basis, as illustrated by Harvard's rule of not accepting on a corporate basis grants or contracts involving "classified research" while leaving individual faculty free to engage in such work if they so desire.

Technocratic education is the latest thing in the universities, and may well come to dominate all other norms. It is a cousin of disciplinary education, but its patterns and purposes are very different. In a disciplinary context, the utility of knowledge is based largely on whether it makes an advance in knowledge already possessed by the discipline and defined by the prevailing theories and framework within the discipline. The criterion would be advances in cognitive order, whether that be measured by increased predictive power or an intuitive satisfaction that one thing makes several other things fit somewhat better. Utility in a technocratic education is measured by the capacity of a body of knowledge to solve a problem in the real world. In a discipline the question is whether reality behaves like the model. In the problem-solving, technocratic context, the question is whether the model behaves like the real world. In the technocratic university, there is even a lot of impressive talk about combining disciplines and training people in "interdisciplinary" ways that make them better than the old kinds of specialists. Behaviorally this may be true, but the purpose of this combining is quite different from the actual effort to combine. The purpose is to make a conceptual apparatus, the very questions of inquiry, fit as closely as possible the lines of operation that are experienced in the real world. Those who are coping with the real world design their problems in a certain way. The purpose of a technocratic education is to define academic knowledge in a way that is as closely parallel as possible to the definitions of those who are actually doing the coping.

It is this parallelism of definition that helps to define the character of the social interest that is served by technocratic education. And this is where the technocratic norm is so different from the others. For, on examination it seems clear that the social interest is not a class in the ordinary sense of the word. The social interest is whatever class or group is at the moment the dominant interest of the regime. The technocratic education, focusing as it does on real social problems, puts the university in an intimate functional relationship with regime, whatever regime one has in mind—federal, local, or nongovernmental or social regime—because problem-solving is a means of maintaining established order, in every sense of the word. If problem-solving is the primary purpose of the regime and the educational system, there is a basis for a high degree of consonance and mutual reinforcement. Moreover, because a regime can have a consciousness and a policy, we have the basis for the kind of conscious, institutional service-rendering that the word "service" has come to imply in dialogues involving the university. Surely this is why "service" has recently become such an important element in the rhetoric of education philosophies.

Technocracy is a relatively new education form, but it accounts for most of the growth in the colleges and universities of the past decade, and more than anything else explains any paradox in the relationship between expanding educational opportunities and expanding student alienation. This new technocratic norm, with its service ethic, has begun to derange at least the first three alternative principles of education. It perceives the educational process itself as part of the conscious service ethic. It tends to define and judge this process in terms of outputs geared to needs in the society rather than in terms of whether knowledge has been expanded. Teaching comes to be viewed as one more problem-solving problem. In our present era, French students were first to perceive the true meaning and significance of this aspect of the problem-solving orientation, though they articulated it rather badly. The Twenty-second of May Movement at Nanterre, which ushered in the 1968 revolution in France, was itself triggered by this issue. Many students had been discouraged from taking sociology and directed toward economics, law, and other subjects more in tune with contemporary national direction as defined by the state examination. These examinations plugged the educational systems and the students into the prevailing definition of needs as handed down by government bureaucracy and major corporations. Classroom obstruction began over objections to the "technocratization of intelligentsia" and the putting of the university in the "service of capitalism." (It seems fairly clear that they really meant the regime, the Establishment, the contemporary order, rather than the specific capitalist enerprises.) This is a fundamental reason, too, why students from the center as well as from the left sought accord with the French workers. All felt that there was a basis for class solidarity between students and workers when students seem to be treated as merely workers-to-be in the new job-oriented and problem-solving orientation of the university. (It should be noted that at the "radical" new Vincennes, extensive student participation in decision-making is unmistakably leading to the American disciplinary pattern of departments, courses, and majors. It is extremely interesting and significant that they are turning to a crude disciplinary pattern as their antidote for the technocratization of the curriculum.)

From this it follows rather obviously to any politically oriented analyst that the technocratic norm of education can only expand in comparison to the other norms of education. Deliberate service to a regime is a market relation of never-ending profit on both sides. One can anticipate the results by looking at a completely different market, the automobile in relation to the New York Port Authority. Charged in 1921 with building a transportation system, the Port Authority built highways because no resistance was offered to them. This led to the decline and fall of the railroads and a completely unbalanced system in the New York area, despite the fact that no policy-maker ever preferred bankrupt railroads.

The University in Mesh

There are many dangers inherent in these patterns, but the greatest danger of all threatens when the new technocratic definition of the purpose of education becomes part of a general movement toward modern totalitarianism without terror. The university was something that was supposed to be out of mesh with the rest of society. If this is the case, the technocratic norm is the end of the university. The problem-solving university, even when the service is supposedly "in balance with research and teaching," is an institution in mesh with all the other institutions in society. This is in fact never denied by the proponents of the service university. For example, shortly on leaving his post as Commissioner of Education, Harold Howe was reported in the press as having warned that it is "at the peril of our society that we seek a return to former isolation. . . ." Inevitably, public servants who are under pressure to do more than their best to solve real problems come to perceive the university as one of their best resources. They are most comfortable when the interchange with scholars is "on the basis of the same vocabulary." They celebrate the emergence of the new schools of public affairs, urban institutes, and so on. Inevitably, the way of the public servant and the corporate executive is made easier when inside the university this problem-solving approach is made systematic and is accepted as virtuous. But this only helps define with special clarity the degree to which the government and the university in the United States have traditionally been on opposite sides of the market. Defining the condition of being in mesh as a virtue is something new. Governments with good intentions—along with faculty and students with their good intentions—become far greater dangers to academic freedom than antiintellectual attacks from the lunatic fringe.

In the midst of controversy over education and what kinds we should espouse, it is amazing how quickly faculty and other educators assume political roles. When their own policies and positions are at stake, they quit being teachers and give up trying to use an educational model to overcome this particular type of controversy even as they continue to use educational models to overcome intellectual controversies in which they themselves are not at issue. But turning to a political model for solving issues involving the educational institution itself almost inevitably involves espousal of a problem-solving, technocratic approach, despite the fact that this has been a major contributor to the very crunch the educators find themselves in. Inasmuch as the universities have been caught red-handed performing all kinds of unsavory services for reactionary interests, it is much easier to agree on a principle of universal service than to insist on terminating the services already being performed. It seems both sophisticated and realistic to admit that service is the name of the game, even though to do so is to abandon any notion of university autonomy.

And the crunch that affects the university across the board also affects the individual disciplines. The response by leaders of disciplines and departmental chairmen has tended to be the same as that of the university-wide administrators and educational philosophers. That is to say, undergoing an identity crisis within their own disciplines, many departmental members abandoned their educational role for a political one, thereby agreeing to the general dismantling of their discipline.

Political Science

Political science is as good an example as any. Traditionally, political science experienced the strain of competing educational norms because of the long tradition of classical and liberal approaches competing with the emerging dominance of the disciplinary definition of the field. Generally this has been a useful and productive interchange, in which the independence of the discipline itself was probably maintained. But in recent years, the cry for relevance and the competition for research monies have combined to favor the emergence of a technocratic element. On the Establishment side of the field, there is talk of schools of public affairs, of urban and other problems, and of the various methods that might make political science a better servant to decent public policy. On the other side, there is the complaint about relevance, meaning relevance to sets of interests in society that would not necessarily be well served by the kinds of adjustments that the established elders in the field might have in mind.

The discipline is now suffering some serious intellectual disorders because both sides to the controversy, though disagreeing at a superficial level, are agreeing on one fundamental adjustment, namely, the expansion of the technocratic aspect of the field. There is no difference in principle between a public affairs school that would serve the government and a school for revolutionists that would serve the next government. Modeling, budgeting, decision-making, and computerization are the technocratizing elements of the established political science, whereas action research, black studies, and various efforts to convert the American Political Science Association into an interest group are the equivalent features of the new left demands. Caught in the middle, and having learned that political models are to be preferred to educational models for settling disputes, the political science leadership will ultimately embrace both sides. The number of problems that any discipline can deal with, if it wishes, is unlimited. At some point along the way, the discipline will have disappeared, but by that time so will the university within which it once operated—unless there is a serious and detached reexamination of the character of the contradictory educational norms and an actual decision as to which ones shall become the central organizational principle of the discipline.

An Era of Irony

This is an era of bitter irony for the independent university. It is ironic that the attack comes from friends rather than enemies of the intellect. It is ironic that the defense will destroy the university just as surely as the attack. It is ironic that the crisis has come at the very time when American society can finally afford an institution that is out of mesh. It is all the more ironic that as the university succeeded in freeing itself from domination by narrow upper classes and their regimes it may buckle under and lose its identity to a more democratic, permissive, and less class-bound regime. All this is happening during a period in which the political norm of pluralism is stressed on the one hand while on the other hand the one best social counterpoise, the alienated intellectual, is suppressed. The final irony is that the alienated intellectual is being suppressed more from within than from without—within himself and within his institution. He is not being suppressed involuntarily at all; he is being suppressed by the ethic of service.

However, ironic as it may be, such an analysis can help clarify the issues and ultimately the positions to be taken by university policy-makers and governmental officials. First, the analysis should make it unmistakably clear that once society's own legitimacy begins to crumble, the university will also be implicated. The tie between university and society is simply too close to have it otherwise. But the message is not coming through yet. The universities have been wrong in the manner of their identification with society in our day. They have been caught red-handed, but nonetheless they have gotten the wrong message. The direction of the response cannot be in terms of a political model in which success is measured by peace and the degree to which students and other opponents have been coopted into currently decadent university ways. But clarification of what kind of institution a given university is could lead to the kind of commitment out of which a real educational approach to the crisis and to the defense of the university can be devised.

Government policy should be derived from the same analysis, though the problem is different, because governments are not universities. The first principle should be, of course, that government shore up universities rather than exploit them. But most government people feel that shoring up is what they are doing now.

Support as Reinforcement

Government demands for university services, even when purchased generously enough to allow a lot of piggyback "pure" research, should be seen simply as a more sophisticated version of century-old agrarian demands for courses in pickle-packing and cherry pie. This ought to be clear enough.

But there is another element of governmental activity that is less explicitly service-oriented but yet may be even more corrosive of the independent university, namely, a policy of blanket and unconditional grants for higher education. An example of this is the recent request of a Carnegie Commission report designing a national program toward the year 2000 (chaired by the perennial Dr. Clark Kerr). The panel expressed eloquently a series of very important sentiments regarding the elimination of race and class barriers and the general desirability of universal access to higher education. But its concerns were entirely with the composition of the student body and the general level of educational quality available both in the universities and preparatory programs. The implication of this, as in most other such reports, is that whenever governments are not involved in highly specific contracts for services, their policies should be kept general and permissive so as to avoid interference. The trouble with this, like any other general delegation of power and resources to an agency or to a private institution or group, is that such a blanket delegation merely reinforces and exaggerates the status quo. Thus, a general and permissive policy of "improving and expanding higher education" is a ticket for total transformation for those universities already in a state of transformation from the disciplinary to the technocratic norm. A policy of "no policy" toward universities is in effect very important because it is an espousal of every compromise and scheming decision that governing university factions make for their universities.

The Moral Basis

Violence in and to the universities, and incessant demands for decentralization, will not end so long as there are students who feel that the university and the regime are in cahoots. This is a prescription for a cure, however, as well as a proposition of cause and effect. Students have succeeded to a great extent because they have been essentially correct in their complaint. They have also succeeded insofar as they have restored the need to provide a moral basis for action. This is all that they can be expected to do, and respect for this part does not lead to acceptance of any program that students might be proposing. Students lack the capacity to state precisely what the moral basis for action should be, but in any case this is a job for America's élites. No élite can possibly be supported if its leaders cannot provide a plausible moral basis for action. An appeal for support on the grounds that they can roll with the punches better than anybody else, and that bargaining is sufficient moral basis in and of itself, is far more corrupt than the refusal of students and dissident faculty to enter into such a bargaining process. University élites have already proven time after time that the results of a wide open bargaining process are not necessarily acceptable. Few college presidents, for example, have rejected a peace-maker role in favor of a real effort to state that essence of the university that cannot be negotiated. It is no wonder that students are ignorant of the nature of the university if those in power in a university are either unwilling or unable to enunciate it.

Rather than face the university crisis by bargaining and risk further loss of legitimacy, it would be far better to try to restore the university to essential principles on which all can agree. Seeking decentralization and participation under present conditions is a solution akin to bleeding by medieval physicians. The patient needs all the blood he has. The only lasting way to solve the so-called power problem is by severance. But, if severance, on what terms?

"Balance," the Learned Societies and the Universities

To anticipate the answer, the American Political Science Association might be taken again as a concrete case in point. Some members of the association are opposed to using it either to serve or to reward service to Congress, state legislatures, or the current programs of given administrative agencies, including the Department of Defense. But what good will the association do if it placates those dissidents by simply adding services to the favorite interests of those dissidents? Would it not be better for all concerned if the association reached for a more essential principle than that of cooption and placation and severed the old activities while resisting new ones? What a great stroke for academic intergrity it would be if the association removed itself from Washington and from those activities that commit it to rewarding certain kinds of public service.

The APSA problem only emphasizes what can hardly be emphasized too strongly, namely, that no solution will ever be found through efforts to strike a balance among interests served or the balance among "research-teaching-service." This analysis has already shown clearly, it seems to me, that service, in the new, technocratic definition, is by and large an unnecessary evil. The analysis also should expose the sophistry of those who talk about research and teaching as though they are separable activities. Research for what? Teaching for what? This questioning takes us back to the five norms of education identified in Table 6–1. In its most ordinary and dull sense, there is research going on in the normal pursuit of each of the ethics identified earlier. Research in the classics might be poring over and rote learning of languages in ancient texts. In the humanities, it may be the prodigious reading of men's ideas and the endless search for their origins. In the problem-solving arena, research is usually the building of a case much as a lawyer would. In the area of practical education, research usually takes the form of experience—field trips and the like, what the new left likes to call "radical research." In the disciplines, research is usually the testing of some guess about cause and effect derived in the latest theoretical fashion. Obviously the question of creating or altering a balance between research and teaching is irrelevant until the emergence of the technocratic norm. Research and teaching are taken as a dichotomy by service- and practice-oriented educators because it is only in these systems where such an issue, particularly leading to the separation of research and teaching, can ever occur. Within the three traditional norms of education—classical, liberal arts, and disciplinary—the idea of research as separate from teaching is absurd. Both are merely aspects of the process of higher learning. The separation being complained about these days comes from the fact that when the problem-solving professors are doing their research they are literally off the campus operating as consultants, in which case they are teaching someone other than their students and their colleagues.

If we are deprived of the opportunity of solving the education crisis by a mere reordering of these three pseudovariables, the remaining alternative is to reexamine basic educational functions themselves. Such a reexamination would, it seems to me, inevitably lead to a severe deemphasis of practical technocratic educational ethics. These ethics not only militate against intellectual life but also against the lower classes. That is, in impact, these systems are basically reactionary. The reactionary aspect of the technocratic education has already been identified. The reactionary aspect of the practical arts education is equally easy to perceive. To the lower classes the university is a vastly important channel of mobility as well as a channel of access to historic knowledge. To equip the lower classes with agricultural and other lesser mechanical skills is simply to equip them all the better to remain in their original class position. It is one thing to offer practical courses for older adults, quite another to offer them on a general community college basis to vast numbers of the white and black working class.

A Way to Independence

This leaves only the first three educational norms within which to develop a proper principle of the university as an independent educator. Of these, disciplinary education seems to be the strongest choice, despite the fact that it leaves a great deal to be desired. First, it can accommodate the other two traditional educational patterns through departmentalization. Second, it is sociologically consonant with the largest educated class. Third, this class is the one into which the more mobile lower classes climb when they move up. Finally, the disciplinary norm is consonant with modern society yet is not in service to it or any particular regime. The disciplinary norm is modern because it works with organized, differentiated knowledge rather than with dilettantish knowledge associated with the classic and the liberal arts education. It is on the other hand generalistic in contrast to the action and service programs, which are by nature particularistic. Therefore, the disciplinary norm is no more a servant to the regime than are the liberal arts or the classical norms. Its opposition to or independence of regimes is reinforced by the fact that scholarship is long-term whereas regime needs are short-term. The purpose of scholarship is cognitive ordering whereas the purpose of action is short-range utility. Disciplinary education equips the individual to serve regimes if he wishes, but it is not institutionally committed to a service concept. Therefore, society pays a minimal price for the long-run, nonparticularistic, professionalized character of disciplinary education. In contrast, the service or technocratic norm is the intellectual counterpart of the neutral civil servant, for it may serve any regime, and further, it has no meaning except in terms defined by its service to some regime.

As long as universities, as corporate entities, serve in this modern sense, there will always be demands to have it serve some other master. This also means that there will be competition both for resources and for power and that the measure of success will be in terms of net growth. It will take a tremendous amount of courage to right the wrongs of recent years by redressing this kind of imbalance and by returning to earlier definitions of the independent university. Most of all, it will take tremendous courage to admit that after Vietnam, the sudden reexpansion of government into domestic affairs may be the worst thing that ever happened to higher education in America. As Andrew Hacker once suggested, we must learn to define the great university president in terms of the number of grants he turns down. Unless standards of restraint are established—*based on a proper sense of what the university must be*—the competition for access to available public monies for education will end up in one of the most disgusting scrambles the country has ever experienced.

7

Yesterday's Revolutionists: The Faculty and the Future of the University

The paradox of expanding education accompanied by increased student and community alienation must be examined more closely inside the university. One can get only so far examining university functions and their relations with the outside world. Many problems in higher education and many solutions in the best long-range interest of the community are found among the views and conduct of the university faculty and administrators. This examination will show why disruption is so easy, why transformation to technocracy is likely, and why true reform is as simple to grasp as it would be difficult to implement. The guiding question is this: If academic freedom and university autonomy are so important, why are so many academic people ready to give them up?

Why Great Universities Are So Susceptible

American academic institutions have enjoyed a long and successful resistance to attacks from the outside world. Generally from

This chapter first appeared in *Midway*, 10, no. 3 (Winter 1970). Copyright © 1970 by the University of Chicago Press.

the traditional right, these attacks have arisen out of distrust of the free, skeptical, godless intellectual. But of whatever ideological hue, the attackers have always seen the university as a source of disorder, discomfort, and alienation and have sought to transform it by instilling it with the spirit of service to God, country, and man.

This old and familiar source of antagonism is now being over-shadowed by another, which comes from within and, in its own mind, from the left. It too is born of distrust of the skeptical, faithless academic, for members of a great university attempt to break new idols as well as old. It is the more serious attack, despite its meager resources, and it is very likely to win out in the end. Facing this new threat, the great universities seem to be playing out a tragedy in which their fate is already determined, because they are now subject to the special and virtually irresistible forces of student privilege, general community antipathy, and, most important, a defenseless faculty. Thus, though external forces may subvert the university, it is likely that the internal dynamics will bring the university still more quickly and more surely to the same end.

The public at large is often mystified by the response of the universities to hostility from within, because it tends not to under-stand the nature of university organization. Contrary to student myths, there is no university power structure. There appears to be one sometimes when a frontal attack involves the university in an outright fight for survival. This is not organization, however, but temporary unity. There is a great deal of central administration, but administration exists for service, not control. The fact is, great universities are extremely susceptible to internal hostilities be-cause they are deliberately not organized. Without a unified and well-organized system of control the university is incapable of dealing efficiently with any demands made on it.

The best example of university nonorganization is in the very area where some of the most serious student demands occur: the power of appointment, promotion, and removal of faculty. The power resides almost completely within the academic departments. Deans and presidents can impose freezes on expansion, but these are general and budgetary powers, not powers of individual appointment. Participation in faculty appointment and promotion passes up through the administrative echelons only in cases of stalemate and bitter indecision with the departments. Student ignorance of this decentralization was never better revealed than during a crisis at Chicago, during January and February of 1969, when the disruption was precipitated entirely by a nonnegotiable demand that the president of the university impose the reappointment of a young, female professor on the Department of Sociology.

A second dimension of university nonorganization against which important student demands are lodged is that of the so-called university commitments to the community. Universities have over the course of years made many evil commitments, and much is due to student agitation that certain commitments have been revealed and discredited. These commitments are sometimes university policy and university decision, but far more often they are commitments that one or another school, department, or individual professor has made with some outside interest. Defense contracts are not entered into by some corporate executive or legislative process. Central university officials review proposed projects if large-scale financing is anticipated, but scrutiny of substantive features of projects is quickly viewed as interference with the freedom of the professor. And here is the point. Many individual professors perform services for the community, and some of these services are not approved by one faction or another. But within the framework of academic freedom it would be impossible to require them to perform these services as part of their university obligation and impossible to inspect all activity to prevent them from performing unwanted services. Such a university would require total mobilization; it would have to inspect all commitments made by individual university personnel in order to assess how each might affect the environment of the university.

The third vital area at issue, in which the nonorganization of the university is also revealed, is that of control over the academic fate of students—passing and failure, ranking and rating. The real powers over such vital decisions are decentralized; student standing is basically a result of multitudes of invidious distinctions made by individual professors and recorded by automatic administrative routine. By and large these demands amount to pressure for a presidential decision to prevent professors throughout the university from making judgments about students or, once made, from recording them.

Passed thus in review, these three dimensions of university organization against which most militant demands are lodged reveal the real dilemma of the great universities in the United States today. Most demands hit the university as a corporate entity when only a part of the university is directly involved. But whether the institution or only a part is involved, universities cannot respond to most of the demands without altering their basic nature. Because there is no unified power structure, universities can rarely literally sit down at the bargaining table if the resulting compromise cannot implemented. It is difficult enough under the most peaceful conditions to authorize representatives to bargain for the entire institution. In moments of crisis, this is rendered virtually impossible. The university is simply not a community in any corporate sense of the word. A university is not a business, government, or trade association. It can rarely speak with one voice—nor should it.

Among the great universities, where did bargaining actually take place during the crisis of the late 1960s? At Harvard? The university felt itself so weak that it could think of nothing but turning itself over to the care of the civil authorities. At Columbia? A total shambles. At Cornell? Only Henry Fielding can capture that tragicomedy: "He would have ravished her had she not, by a timely compliance, prevented him." Even at Chicago, where President Levi and his council and deans showed extraordinary strength, the relation with the students took the form of resolutely doing nothing during the 1969 crisis.

Whatever the university does as a whole, the final course of adjustment amounts to about the same thing. Once the noise subsides the crisis is not over; it transfers itself to the real power centers. When the university representatives make serious blunders, acting inconsistently or revealing cowardice, for example, the militants and their sympathizers can dominate the ensuing discussions. There has been talk at Cornell of "constituent assemblies" and "sovietizing," whereas at Chicago student-faculty committees, Whittely councils, and other arrangements have sprung up. But the point remains that serious implementation takes place at the departmental level and below, over a long period of time, or it does not take place at all—unless by a sudden coup the university administration centralizes the power of decision-making in order to deal directly with the student militants. It may be ironic but it is nonetheless true that though students speak of participation and decentralization, most of their demands would require the very opposite if they were seriously implemented.

Why Students Are So Influential

In the great universities the special character of nonorganization is matched by the special status of students. Students constitute an especially privileged class, and no amount of identification with the underprivileged can change that fact. In the university, perhaps for the only time in his life, the student is given an opportunity to "be someone else" for awhile, or perhaps forever. He is encouraged to experiment with new thoughtways and life styles. He is not deterred from trying new moralities. He may do nothing for long stretches; he is in effect the only adult who is expected to waste time productively. He receives a special status in law—a fact few appreciate unless once involved in some of the bargaining between deans and civil authorities. These and other privileges have been extended over the years, first to include larger and larger numbers of the "square" colleges and then to include larger and larger areas of behavior in each and every college. The old university role, in *loco parentis,* is dying almost everywhere.

Student privilege is as much a part of the university system as academic freedom. The student body and the faculty are each a privileged class. Each class depends on the other, and each class has the power, if it is willing to pay the price, to take away the privileges of the other. The agony of the university arises from the fact that increasing numbers of students are willing to pay the price. The unquestioned privilege of students coupled with the limited capacity of the university to negotiate has rendered the university ripe for disruption and transformation.

Disruption, however, is too general a term. It masks the very special effects student disruptive influence has on the university, for, ironically, the unquestionably good work of the university is far easier to disrupt than the shadier, more dubious work. Students develop contempt for what is familiar; they seize what is nearby. This means disruption of ordinary teaching and scholarship.

They seize an administration building, which exists primarily for maintenance of ordinary college labors—salaries, wages, grades, transcripts, scholarships, and so on. And with no difficulty whatsoever, students can strike out at their social science classes, drop a stink bomb in the hallway, and in many other ways render any kind of intellectual activity impossible. If only to emphasize the extreme delicacy of the best of university life, as well as the student ignorance of it, a number of well-meaning Cornellians offered to protect the professors who dissented from the university's capitulation so that these professors could continue safely to meet their classes.

In contrast, those university activities and commitments that require—to say the very least—considerable justification are far more remote from the students and have usually remained untouched by demonstrations. Labor relations schools, business schools, institutes for defense analysis, programs for the production of prettier apples, training schools for glorified hotel clerks, training programs for producing trained and loyal technocrats, and so on draw their sustenance directly from their own clientele. They may pay the university between 30 and 60 percent "overhead costs," but otherwise they stand as sanctuaries from university as well as student communities. Students usually know very little of these service institutions. Only the Vietnam War exposed a few of them, and these have been opposed primarily for reasons that have to do only with the unpopularity of that war. The Chicago student demonstrators showed their disapproval of university relations with the ghetto by seizing the Center of Urban Studies though the housing office and the major private realtors sat only a few blocks away. Columbia students seized Fayerweather Hall and a few benign social scientists and they disrupted activity around the "arts quad" and library. Meanwhile, practically across the street and undisturbed were several autonomous service institutes whose teaching roles have been to a great extent limited to providing policy consultation to public agencies and officials. A great deal of Columbia's faculty talent has been lost in these autonomous institutes in the past decade.

Even the ROTC issue is the exception that proves the rule. Of the thousands of pseudocourses and nonscholarly appointments existing in the university, the demonstrators pick the one that, after complete abolition, they or their successors in a few years will probably agitate to restore, for, after Vietnam, the political value of civilian officers will again loom large. In any event, the intellectual quality of most advanced courses in ROTC is far greater by any standard than the physical education, home economics, recreation, and other practical arts subjects, which have not come in for any militant action at all. In seizing what is available and familiar, the students, in fact, have been dealing with university misdemeanors while felonies have gone unpunished.

Why Students Will Get Community Support

The university is all the more susceptible to influence because there will always be a considerable amount of community support for student militants when they oppose the basic mission of the university. That mission is not to be the alternative Establishment but to provide the opportunity and the atmosphere in which alternative conceptions and establishments in all fields might be formulated. Because community supporters are respectable and disapprove of disorder, their support takes the form of "while we do not condone their methods . . . ," but it nevertheless is forthcoming. Business has long felt the university to be irrelevant; this is why there are business schools and hotel schools attached to the universities. Agriculture even earlier saw the university as an opportunity and its aloofness as a threat. Government officials and politicians, partly out of sympathy for their richer constituents and partly out of sincere personal conviction, traditionally have been impatient with the separateness and aloofness of the university. Only a shock such as Sputnik could get Washington into education, but even so it mainly emphasized the sciences in the curriculum and created a number of policy-oriented programs. Increasingly, government programs are predicated on direct co-optation of the universities. Many of the autonomous institutes within the university are the result of a crash program of government support following some foreign or domestic crisis. The urban field, for example, is now coming in for its crash program, and all sorts of problem-solving urban institutes and urbanologists are being created with the help of public funds. As of 1969–1970, urban fellowships provided by HUD are being limited entirely and exclusively to graduate students who will sign affidavits guaranteeing that they will go into some form of public service and quite explicitly not into teaching and scholarship.

Despite differences of style, dress, technique, and vocabulary, the new student movements share some quite fundamental values with the respectable elements of the community. They share a discomfort about the aloofness of the university. At bottom this amounts to a basic antagonism to theory, a deeply antiintellectual impatience with academic efforts to distort reality by imposing a logical order on it. It is a grand American tradition, for example, to consider theory and practice as opposites. It is a grand American tradition to hallow the immediate utility of knowledge. Americans were the first existentialists. Experience comes from action, and knowledge comes from experience. It seems useless to insist with students or their older colleagues in the community that the effort to accumulate experience is no longer experience itself but, in fact, theory-building. Students no longer buy the argument that a good theory is far more radical than a movement to abolish hunger in the neighborhood, that a good theory is better than reality if it shapes reality. The desire for service seems to be stronger than the credibility or attractiveness of the life of the mind.

For many years the great universities of the United States have stood as an ongoing (though incomplete) revolution, despite the antagonism of the entire community. The practice of even partial autonomy for the university is a spectacular achievement, appreciated by anyone with any knowledge of other countries or of the nineteenth-century United States. Academic freedom, the autonomy of the organized disciplines, the value of cognitive order over utility (that is, the usefulness of useless knowledge), all represent tentative and not very popular victories against the forces of relevance and service. Despite the immensely beneficial results of university autonomy, the revolution is incomplete because nobody except the professoriat has ever been very enthusiastic about the arrangement. Governments and the public oppose the student movement these days primarily because of the disorder, not because of the student goals. Administrators are continually finding it necessary to justify the university in terms of the services it renders, the "community resources" to be found there, the problem-solving capacities to be used there. The very word "academic" as it is used in our vocabulary is quite revealing of community values. So is the word "trivial," from "trivium," which before our age referred to the three purely academic subjects—grammar, rhetoric, and logic.

Very early in the decade of expansion the student militants joined *Life* and other popular media in a concerted attack on such doctrines as "publish or perish," as though publishing debased both the man and the subject. Student demands for participation in faculty appointments is largely a means of ensuring the relevance of faculty performance to the prevailing definition of relevance. "Good teaching" is a criterion beyond the control of the specialized disciplines and easily accessible to the lay community. It is also a criterion that can be easily adjusted to the two-to-four-year cycle of public taste. Even the student attack on university services runs with the grain of community prejudice. Attacks on services to war industries and the like are not meant to end service orientation as such but are aimed at maintaining and expanding this orientation. The bone of contention is not the existence of ties to any establishment but merely the particular establishment the university is going to serve.

Thus, the student movement will attract significant community support because the militant represents a counterrevolution, not a revolution. There is no basic principle that distinguishes the current student demands from the long-standing demands of farmers, businessmen, and labor leaders for practical subjects and immediate results. There is no ethical principle by which to distinguish university-sponsored services to business or farm interests from services to the poor in the ghetto. The current zeal reflects the popular culture. It represents a betrayal of what was thought to be a well-established student-faculty coalition to preserve the academic privilege of experimentation and to prevent administrators and trustees from selling out to community demands for the very large dividends that accrue to those who want to convert universities into multiversities comprised of indistinguishable social service agencies. It is all too clear that the student movement would never have had a chance if its behavior were revolutionary.

Nor would the student agitation have had a chance if its behavior were a case of license. But the issue was never a question of liberty versus license, or freedom versus responsibility. The privilege of academic status for students is license. License contained within the university is exactly what academic freedom is, and there can be little academic freedom for faculty without this systematic license for students. The student movement is, therefore, especially influential because it represents an effort to give up privilege. This is the most effective part of the students' revolution: It is counterrevolution. The militants get tremendous support from the central mass of students when they cry out against the institutional racism of a university encouraging Greek and teaching functionalist theory in social science "when people out there are starving." The vulgar existentialist proposition, that the best knowledge is gained through action, is offered as further justification—and that sounds shockingly like such old hard-headed anti-intellectualisms as the "school of hard knocks" and "experience is the best teacher" that always found favor in the community. But the movement's real effectiveness lies in sacrifice. Privilege in any form is undemocratic, and the students demand their democratic right as citizens to abolish their own privileges by abolishing the principle of university independence altogether. Behind the beards is a point of view that the community will ultimately embrace.

Why the Faculty Will Contribute to Its Own Undoing

The liberal tradition has always seemed vital for free inquiry in the university. But after two or more generations of partially successful revolution, misunderstanding of the requirements of liberalism has made it the fatal flaw in the defensive armor of academic freedom. Liberalism has become soft and deranged. It has changed its order of priorities by putting the process of bargaining above all other values, and in the process, it has forgotten one of the basic nonnegotiable commitments of the strong liberal regime—in the words of Kurt Lewin, a steadfast "intolerance of intolerance."

Liberals in the university have no problem handling demands that originate from their right. This helps explain why outside threats are no longer so menacing. Conservative forces inside academia are also dealt with firmly. If a delegation of students were to call on a social science department chairman to demand a better presentation of Christianity, they would be sent away with a firm lecture on the evils of interfering with who teaches what. This is not to say that every conservative demand is rejected outright. Conservatives are dealt with rationally and with restraint.

Demands that issue from the left, however, are an entirely different matter. The liberal, after years of identifying with the left, quite frankly cannot distinguish a good demand from a bad one. He is ready to abandon organized knowledge itself if that seems to be the only manner of proving that no one can outlib him, for the voices of the left remove his bearings. The liberal in academia faces right with forthrightness and honesty. He faces left with hypocrisy.

In the midst of a severe confrontation at Chicago over the very question of control over faculty, a group of nearly fifty social scientists, several distinguished scholars among them, could suggest that the entire structure was almost as illegitimate as the militants charged:

The partial insulation of academic life from the exigencies of everyday life . . . entails the danger that the members of universities will not be responsive to the needs for change. . . . Many of us faculty members are resistant to change, for we have become adapted to the existing structure and find it easier to continue work within it than to adjust to a new one.

Thus, rather than deal with the demands as such, they were able only to express a general mea culpa. A larger group signed a petition two months later demanding a change in the appeal procedure for the discipline of some of the demonstrators at a time almost precisely calculated to cast a pall of illegitimacy over the entire disciplinary process. Almost none of the signers had attended any of the disciplinary hearings, but most were quick to agree with student criticisms of the process. The chairman of the Committee on Human Development, an interdepartmental curriculum seriously involved in the 1969 Chicago crisis, went still further by admitting at the outset that

the participation of students . . . has been less than it should be, and
. . . that participation should increase . . . regarding the student role
in curriculum planning, faculty selection and evaluation, examinations,
research criteria, and possibly [other areas] of which I am yet unaware.

The Harvard administration responded to the black student crisis
by allowing students to help choose their own professors in black
studies but not elsewhere in the university. This will create a new
university ghetto, and even so, the extension of the principle of
faculty submission will not be easy to limit. By such compromising
action, the Harvard faculty has forced itself into the dilemma of an
ultimate choice between admitting it created a ghetto and extending the principle of faculty dependence throughout the university.

The important point here is that such actual and proposed
surrenders enjoy widespread faculty support. Cornell in particular
proves that almost any student movement to dismantle the structure of academic, professorial independence—as long as it comes
from left-sounding voices—can recruit important faculty support
in rather large numbers. Professors who are good analysts, especially social scientists, also make excellent rationalizers. They are
guilt-ridden because at one and the same time there are grave ills
in the university that need correcting and certain things about
which no negotiation can be possible; they proceed to write the
poetry for retreat hoping that the collective wisdom of the student
body will ultimately save the faculty from its own weaknesses. To
the militant, the university can prove its honesty only by creating
its own counterheroes, its own countermyths, in effect a complete
counterestablishment. Somehow the liberal mind enters into discourse of such a kind in the spirit of liberalism. Yet it cannot
escape the dilemma. It can never let the students have their complete victory, but negotiation ending in anything short of victory
can never, to the students, appear as anything but two-faced.

Faculty liberals express a certain kinship with the student
spokesmen and feel some confidence in negotiation. For their part,
the militants seem to feel no kinship in return, for they are as
contemptuous of negotiation generally as they are of the Estab-

lishment which must do the negotiating. During the crisis at Chicago in 1969, the provost appointed an ad hoc faculty committee to review the social science dean's decision to refuse a second three-year appointment for the aforementioned professor. On the eve of that committee's decision, one of the faculty voices of the Chicago student movements seriously proposed before the college faculty meeting that it pass a resolution supporting the ad hoc committee only if the committee recommended reversal of the dean's decision.

The new social conscience of the student reasons according to its own unique system of logic. For example, students argue constantly that because disruption is a political act, student militants should be given amnesty. Any attempt to impose discipline or in any way defend the institution is political suppression. The most extreme position, which owing to repetition no longer sounds either very extreme or illogical, is that because things are not right in society at large, the academic way of life must be replaced by "a more humane institution, whose priorities are people, not abstract knowledge." Strangely enough, such reasoning attracts hundreds of faculty in major universities throughout the country. Intellectuals in any field ought to perceive and be repelled by such severe violations of rules of logic and ethics. But logic itself has come to be perceived as a weapon of suppression, and the liberal spirit today reacts with extreme fear and guilt to anything suspected of suppression. Cornell University has had one of the most advanced and enlightened disciplinary systems among colleges in the United States. Many a demonstration elsewhere has been dedicated to achieving an ideal that still falls short of Cornell's reality. But this did not prevent the entire Cornell system from becoming implicated in the crisis of April 1969. Capitulation to the black students, including an agreement to change the existing disciplinary system as part of an ordinary bargaining process, implies that the university felt itself to be illegitimate.

But faculty liberalism does not merely accept the illogical in the movements. Faculty liberalism also accepts the totalitarian values espoused by the militants. This totalitarian strain has nothing to do with the fancy for left-wing words. Militants are neither left nor right when they seek to make all social institutions alike. Totalitarianism is a simple phenomenon of being forcibly in mesh. Totalitarian values are those that are impatient with institutions not working shoulder to shoulder in some common cause. Totalitarian policies are those that seek to provide systematic directions, sanctions, and incentives to put all institutions in mesh. In mass democracies, many institutions are, mostly voluntarily, in mesh. But it is in these very mass democracies that being out of mesh is such an important function for the best universities to perform. Universities must be a balance wheel, not a cog wheel. It is incredible that all academic personnel do not immediately see government and student and other public claims as basic and fundamental threats to the independence of the university and to the true public service that a great university is obliged to perform. That true public service is the simple act of being systematically out of mesh.

Being out of mesh with institutions and out of joint with the times ought, of course, to begin with the severance of services to war and to technocratization, just as the students argue. But the correctness of their critique is matched by the incorrectness of their current demands, for they are at bottom no more interested in maintaining the independence of the university than are the other elements of the public outside the university. Collectively, the faculty has been unable to come to grips with this. The faculty, those revolutionists of yesterday, desperately need to recollect what it was they and their predecessors were revolutionary about.

Why the Future Depends on Administrators

Having eliminated itself from real contention, the faculty, ironically, leaves the field to university administrations and administrators. This is indeed a sorry fate, but unexpected abdications rarely produce delightful alternatives. Nonetheless, some of the most recent crises seem to bear out this simple yet fundamental fact. When the university president, his deans, and his councils show strength and judgment, the university survives. When these same functionaries exhibit weakness, the university loses. University authorities can be weak in different ways. They can be weak as they were at Cornell and capitulate without a how-be-you. The faculty will then provide the appropriate rationalizations. Or, they can be weak as at Harvard and turn the university over to the civil authorities. The 1969 Chicago reaction is an example of strength. The authorities at Chicago do not represent some kind of a mean between the two extremes of weakness at Cornell and Harvard. The Chicago 1969 pattern is in fact noncomparable. The officials there simply behaved according to their grasp of what an academic institution is and ought to be.

Taking all the values of academic freedom more seriously than many faculties, the Chicago administrators in 1969 refused to budge on the demands of those who occupied their offices. Because they had no particular power, these administrators simply refused to communicate except to reiterate their position that the university can impose no solutions on departments or individual professors and that there was nothing to talk about as long as the business of the university was being disrupted. Ultimately the sit-in spent itself not from exhaustion, expulsion, or boredom but from the awareness that it could never gain a broad enough basis of support among the student body and faculty unless the university co-operated by making some horrible blunder. Negotiation was never really the goal anyway. The leaders in fact escalated their demands as the days wore on. They then tried "guerrilla action," making spot attacks on well-known persons or places, seeking to encourage blunders. Blunders give the militants the confirmation they need not merely to expand student support but to resolve the faculty sense of guilt in their favor. Faculty guilt during the crisis at Chicago took the form of searching desperately for flaws in the disciplinary process. Faculty guilt had far more with which to assuage itself at Harvard and Cornell.

But even at Chicago the administrators cannot prevent faculty and departments from budging. The sad fact is, a strong administration can save the university from the student onslaught, but it cannot save the faculty from itself.[1] Faculties that must be left free to stand rigidly with their disciplines and their professional standards are also faculties that are free to compromise and "prove their relevance" in almost any way they see fit. With increasing frequency, faculty appointments are being made according to student tastes. More and more frequently faculty appointments are being made according to the balancing strategy once associated with political ticket makers. Course credit is increasingly being given for work supervised by unqualified persons or for work that does not qualify as academic. Means are being fashioned to give students more official roles in choosing faculty. (It is difficult to guess which faculty member or candidate will be first to volunteer to turn over his entire dossier to students. But if students are to have an official role and yet not see the dossiers, their second-class citizenship would be even more apparent than before they had any official role.) Finally, presidents and deans cannot stop the creation of institutes and special services, and usually would not want to stop them even if they could. So, along with the services the universities already perform for classes in retreat will be added those to suit classes on the march. There is not going to be any severing of university ties with society, but only a strengthening of them.

This is the form defeat will take. When the crises are all over, universities will have been transformed. The transformation will be a fulfillment of the hopes that the community always had—

[1] Take for example the Chicago reaction of 1970. Student hysteria over the Cambodian incursion and the Kent State disaster brought the faculty to its knees. The governing faculty council passed fancy resolutions condemning the war, establishing it as the cause of the Kent student deaths and injuries, providing the grade of pass for those in good standing who wanted to take the remainder of the term for political action, and setting aside a two-week recess prior to the 1970 elections for door-knocking. In so doing, the faculty had given the lie to its own famous commitment to academic freedom. But here is another case where the outcome depends on the administrators. The president had held to a strong line in 1969. In 1970 he counseled weakness.

easier access to all standards of excellence and immediate service from all sources for all needs. And the changes sought will not have been seriously opposed, because a faculty committed ideologically to change has become incapable of distinguishing one change from another.

PART IV

LAW AND THE
USES OF DISORDER

8

Law versus Leadership: Institutionalized Change versus the Iron Law of Decadence

Revolutions in technology, in population growth, and in egalitarianism provided a cascade of public problems in our time. There was a tremendous increase in demands for change and a tremendous increase in calls for leadership to make movements and to give effect to those demands. There was also a tremendous increase in the call for public authority, to institutionalize the changes.

But institutionalized change sounds like a contradiction in terms. Leadership and public authority are associated, particularly in a time of change; but they do not necessarily associate comfortably. How can the need for a dynamic society and dynamic leadership be reconciled with good public authority, which requires law and regularity? How can change be institutionalized without running afoul of the iron law of decadence? There are no pat answers. But useful responses lie somewhere in the relationship between law and leadership.

Putting Leadership in Its Place

Leadership looms very large in contemporary democracies—especially in America. Despite our tradition of individualism and egalitarianism, there is a strong strain of leadership. These traits are inconsistent and contradictory, but people in collectivities do not look for consistency. They want solace, and solace seems to be achieved by having one's individuality and giving it up at the same time.

The leadership bias is built into the culture. About the highest compliment paid a youngster is "He's a leader." Recommendations for college speak of leadership qualities. To be thought of as not a leader is to have a bleak future.

Of course there are different types and kinds of leaders, and some distinctions must be made. Some leaders are style setters. One can be a leader by being the best of a type—a leader in sports is the standard-bearer against whom others are measured. In professions and in skilled labor, the leader, as in sports, represents sought-after skills. A leader in fashions sets future tastes.

But obviously these are not the meanings of leadership that figure large in the writing of American history or theories of democracy. The leadership quality that is imbedded deep in our history has to do with leadership as a political function. Here we do not mean leadership as symbolic of those qualities of excellence and achievement that are worthy of emulation. Leadership in this functional sense is neither role nor symbol nor criterion. Leadership in this sense is an activity performed by some people on others—a relationship in which one expects to be influenced. I am a leader, or perhaps *the* leader, if because of me people expect to do things they would not do were it not for my urging—that is, my leadership. Leadership in this classic sense is thus a relationship of expected influence between people. In a collective situation it is, therefore, a function, because in informal situations people depend on it to carry out some common task.

Obviously in a large and complex society, especially one in which so few people have any personal familiarity with other people, leadership is indispensable. A collection of individuals can get together on a task through discussion like a group of Quakers, or by drawing lots, or by turning to a soothsayer. But these are very inefficient alternatives, especially in large aggregates; moreover, even the decision as to the method of getting together requires some leadership. In any collectivity, the separation of the leadership function is the first division of labor.

That being granted, however, the question remains: How important should leadership be in a large political democracy? To grant leadership as a social fundamental is not to accept it unqualifiedly as an essential governmental function. Yet, we have transformed it precisely in this manner.

How important has leadership really been in our scheme of self-government? After all, we should certainly not fear attacking and losing something if we never had much of it anyway.

One could look at the full sweep of nearly 200 years of self-government and find that actually we have had very little national leadership. So little have we had that any pupil in American history can name most of the top leaders, and many of these on closer examination will be found to be scoundrels rather than leaders. Alexis de Tocqueville names no leaders in his great and classic study of American democracy during the 1830s. He was much more struck by the large number of local associations and small-time nongovernmental leaders and found in these the secret of American democracy. Nearly seventy years later another foreign observer, Lord Bryce, wrote an essay entitled "Why Great Men Are Not Chosen Presidents." And Max Weber took the rarity of respectable leaders as a mark of the vocation of politics in America.

Or, let us look at Congress. We have had so few leaders in Congress that we can almost boast that Congress has "solved the problem of leadership." Congress has, quite seriously, solved the problem of leadership with functional specialization in committees and elective parliamentary offices. The average congressman is a rather dull man. He cooperates; he is a good committee worker. In an address to freshman congressmen, Mr. Sam Rayburn once summed up the matter with his now-famous advice, "If you want to get along, go along." This, not initiative, is what the congressman is socialized to.

The same is true in the Senate, despite its somewhat more grandiose reputation. In his massive *U.S. Senators and Their World,* Donald Matthews concluded that most senators not only hold hard work and specialization as the highest virtues, they also voluntarily put a great deal of pressure on senators who would be leaders "before their time" and "out of their element."[1] The very distinction between "club member" and "outsider," which makes up so much of the so-called atmosphere of the Senate, rests on the obedience to the rule of cooperation and clubbiness. Senators yield to each other overwhelmingly in terms of the respect each accords to the other for the specialization and confidential knowledge he has gained in committee work. Note that only one thin volume was required to record all our *Profiles in Courage.* Or, in recent years, compare the low Senate influence of such leaders as Estes Kefauver and Robert Kennedy to the contrasting situations of such club men as John Sparkman and Edward Kennedy.

As early as 1885, in his classic book *Congressional Government,* Woodrow Wilson could lament the decline of leadership in the Congress. But was that warranted? All he could truly lament was the decline of some of the great debates that occasionally took place between such people as Webster, Clay, and Calhoun. But in no early period were there many leaders or great debates to put on the list as evidence for Wilson's lament. And how would it be if we ever enjoyed the mythical situation that Wilson felt that we had declined from? One look at the U.N. General Assembly

---

[1] Donald R. Matthews, *U.S. Senators and Their World* (Chapel Hill: University of North Carolina Press, 1960), especially pp. 92–102; and Ralph Huitt, "The Outsider in the Senate," *American Political Science Review,* Vol. 55 (1961), pp. 566 ff.

will suggest what happens when every man considers himself an autonomous actor.

Because congressmen are not leaders they are not therefore merely followers. One of the weaknesses of the notion of leadership is that it fosters a false dichotomy. The absence of a lot of leadership in a functioning institution may simply suggest that the institution functions well whether there is leadership or not.

Lyndon Johnson is a good illustration of the limits of leadership. In the Senate, his effectiveness was very largely owing to his official role as majority leader—an office from which he derived certain powers—rather than some personal characteristics of leadership Johnson the man bore in his magical gladstone bag. Indeed, Johnson was more effective than most in that job. But a recent study by John Stewart indicates that Mike Mansfield has been almost as effective—and no one thinks of him as a leader.[2] Like the old party bosses, the Senate leader is powerful and effective by virtue of his office; and each holds the office only to the extent that he holds a majority of the Senate members of his party, in the one case, or the war leaders, in the other. In fact most powerful political leaders have deliberately avoided the outward trappings and traits of leadership when they have run governments. No man was more gray and diffident than the typical Tammany boss.

Unfortunately for Johnson, he forgot these limits and conditions when he went to the presidency. Probably he had read too many history and political science texts; but for whatever reason, he came to the erroneous conclusion that the presidency is an office for leaders and, by definition, held by leaders and run by leadership. What he found, in fact, was that the presidency offers only rare opportunities or demands for leadership and that the rest of the time is for official use of the office for formulating and executing policies. What he thought constituted leadership was in part the prestige that inheres in the office. And for the remainder, what we as well as he thought was his leadership turned out most of

[2] John Stewart, *Independence and Control: The Challenge of Senatorial and Party Leadership,* Ph.D. dissertation, University of Chicago, 1968.

the time to be nothing but his vigorous support of values already established as public policy or public commitment. When a few active minorities expressed doubt in the policies or attacked the implementation of them, Johnson found that leadership was misery, for what appeared to be leadership in a bullish market turned out in a bearish market to be responsibility.

Johnson is, in fact, quite comparable to Herbert Hoover, despite extreme differences in style and self-conception. Both men were unusually well equipped for office—better indeed than any other presidents of this century. Each man was elected to office by the overwhelming support of his party and the electorate. And in the face of crisis, both applied with uncommon zeal, sincerity, and skill the so-called principles of leadership they had acquired through years of experience. Both of them failed, but not owing to any tragic characterological flaw (suggested of Johnson by Eric Goldman) or to betrayal (probably suspected by Johnson). They failed because they applied principles of leadership to a government that had become anachronistic. They were fit, of course, but they had become fit in an unfit fitness. So much for their leadership.

One could go so far as to say that our political parties deliberately eliminate leadership qualities. Most of our memorable leaders emerge during periods of crisis, when recruitment processes tend to get a little loose and the way of a charismatic leader is suddenly made easier. The rest of the time such people are usually discouraged from political roles and end up becoming evangelists, individual entrepreneurs, or just plain unhappy people. One of the reasons why so many spectacular leaders and demagogues have come from the South is because the South traditionally has had weaker parties, and therefore fewer institutional means of preventing leadership from coming to the top.

The same is true elsewhere in organized societies. In the life of most large businesses, leadership is actually a one-time thing, a period through which a business passes before it has regularized its means of developing more predictable and effective procedures.

W. C. Durant was a great leader without whose qualities General
Motors would hardly exist today. But he held that office for a
scant seven years, and was succeeded by Alfred P. Sloan, not a
leader but an organization genius, who hold the top post for
twenty-three years. Likewise in unions, in the early stages there is
leadership. Later in the life of a union you get job classification,
contract administration, and the other functions for which the
union actually exists in order to serve its members.[3]

What this suggests is that the genius of American democracy
has not been its leaders but the capacity of its ordinary people to
contrive institutions that work for them.

Leadership in Government: The Deadly Virtues

In order to provide an antidote for leadership, this argument has
obviously gone too far the other way. Leadership is an indispensable element in society. The point is, it is indispensable but
limited to certain stages and phases of the social process, and like
any other technique or methods, it can all too quickly be overdone.
Clearly it is overdone when our dependence on it leads us to accept
extant institutions and simply wait around for the right leadership
to come along to make the institutions work. This is a little like
the mythical Western settlers who waited for the troops to inter-
vene and save them from the Indians. This view of society, which
depends so much on leadership, really does reduce society from
the true drama it is to cheap melodrama.

To be quite concrete, leadership most clearly reaches its limits
in the governmental stage of the social process. That is to say,
leadership may be vital in the democratic social process; but this
is a pregovernmental reality. Leadership leads; it does not govern.

[3] See Chapters 1 and 2.

Consider the major characteristics of leadership: Leadership galvanizes, energizes, unifies, and focuses demands. It evokes dedication; it brings people out from their private shells. There would be little real public opinion without leadership. Leadership is unpredictable. You cannot count on it emerging when you need it. You cannot predict exactly what directions leaders will pursue, and you cannot predict exactly what impact leadership will have on the system or organization within which it emerges.

All these characteristics are desirable; they are actually what we mean when we speak proudly of a dynamic or open society. Innovation is inconceivable without them. In fact, without leadership we would have no problems, and we should be proud of our problems. No country has more. Compare us to Spain or to Saudi Arabia. Problems are in the eye of the beholder. They are a matter of definition. A society without a constant sense of being in trouble is a dead society, and leaders are what enliven it.

Now turn to the same qualities in government. With Shaw, suddenly all these virtues of leadership become deadly virtues. True, governments, especially in modern mass societies, need a few leaders. But to design institutions so that they depend on leaders to make them work is to court disaster—either the disaster of dying for lack of leaders at the appropriate time or the disaster of dying for having just one too many leaders at the wrong time—that is, the dictator who emerges following the collapse of the capacity of government institutions to do anything. Just as the old cartoon said of heroes, dictators are made, not born. We invent them.

The intervention-of-the-troops factor is quite truly at work here. Why should we look critically at our institutions and seek to reform them if good leadership intervenes just in time to turn the trick? And this picture of our present faith in the intervention of this royal mounties factor is not overdrawn. A perusal of almost any major American government textbook will reveal a tendency to treat the presidency in terms of its leadership demands and capacities. The leading work on the presidency, by Professor Neustadt of Harvard, is entitled *Presidential Power: The Politics of Leadership*.[4] Treatments in textbooks are usually entitled "presidential leadership."

These views are not factually incorrect. But the particular stress is distorted, the distortion has consequences, and when we check the consequences, we can see why there is need to revive a tradition of distrust in the leadership factor. Leadership promotes unity when government seeks to separate. Politics may need unity to get a majority vote; but thereafter the law distinguishes among categories, separates out violators or beneficiaries. In sum, government must make choices, authoritative choices, and this is inevitably a disunifying factor.

Second, leadership seeks dependence, whereas government, especially democratic self-government, seeks *in*dependence, such that each individual can relate to others and to government on the basis of his individual rights and obligations as a citizen. A healthy person gives up identity to a leader and a movement or campaign in order to have a better individual situation afterwards. Preference for unity as a constant state of affairs is sick, oppressive, undemocratic.

Third, and most important in its applicability to the crises of the 1960s and 1970s, leadership is inconsistent. Here most clearly the virtue of social unpredictability has become a vice in a governmental context. Take civil rights policy as an example. The force and effectiveness of civil rights legislation can be found only in the South. *This is a direct result of depending on leadership rather than law to make our governmental institutions work*. The presidency, under Democrats or Republicans, is an urban institution, therefore a Northern industrial institution. When we give the president discretion rather than direct him by law, this discretion makes him personally responsible for the results of his own decisions; under such conditions, he cannot take responsibility for altering his own constituency.

And look at the consequences of this leadership. The most

[4] (New York: John Wiley, 1960.)

recent figures for 1968–1969 show the following record: In Illinois, there was very little more desegregation than in the Southern states. Thus, 13.6 percent of the black children in Illinois were attending schools in which the majority of pupils were white as opposed to 8.3 percent in Alabama, 8.9 percent in Louisiana, and 6.7 percent in Mississippi. Worse yet, in Chicago during the same period, the rate was less than half that of Alabama. Only 3.2 percent of Chicago's black students were attending schools in which a majority of students were white, and 85 percent of Chicago's black children attended schools 95 percent or more segregated.

In an important sense, then, the past four presidents used leadership in the North and law in the South, when, ironically, they might have achieved just and lasting progress in the civil rights field the other way around. That is, in the South the president could have led a personal educational campaign because the South is not his constituency; and he should have, because the South needed to be unified with the rest of the country and shown how changes through law in race relations would not destroy its way of life. The presidency could have been, in Teddy Roosevelt's words, the "bully pulpit" in the South. In contrast, any of our presidents should have used law in the North because (1) presumably there was more support and less need of educational campaign and (2) because law would have removed this issue from his personal responsibility in the eyes of constituency. ("Mayor Daley, I've got no choice. This hurts me more than it does you.")

So, in large part the principle of leadership has helped only to lead into a period of governmental illegitimacy. Inconsistency in government is probably government's most damaging and self-defeating behavior. Senator Stennis, for example, may not have been led by the most exalted of motives, but few have recently served the country better than when he called attention to the inconsistencies in the implementation of civil rights policies. When one considers suburban incorporation and zoning, public housing and urban redevelopment, police practices, school construction and districting, and such quasipublic controls as rest in the hands of local real estate boards, one cannot say that Northern segregation is merely de facto and not the result of the same systematic governmental efforts that have kept the races segregated in the South. The call for consistency should be a call to advance enforcement in the North rather than leave the present pattern or contract it in the South. But this will never be done without recognizing that Northern racism is also de jure and must, as in the South, be attacked by legislative means rather than by leadership.

These inconsistencies that undermine legitimate government are not confined to the one area of civil rights. Inconsistency infects and affects other areas just as much. Administrative leadership, based on the principle of delegation—which in *The End of Liberalism* I call "liberal jurisprudence"—has given us one railway rate historically for east-west relations and another for north-south relations. Such administrative leadership in draft law enforcement has given us the free George Hamiltons and the shackled Cassius Clays. These inconsistencies are made possible by a vague conscription program that leaves the actual choice to local leadership rather than to law.

Administrative leadership has also given us the practice of outright favoritism of established carriers over newcomers in the communications field; and it has given us in the defense areas a policy of favoring big companies over the smaller specialists. Or take one of President Nixon's public relations spectaculars—environmental control. Here clearly is a case where President and Congress are tending to rely on leadership and not law. The act sets up a new Council on Environmental Quality, modeled after the Council of Economic Advisors. The act states a whole lot of lofty sentiments, such as "it is the policy of the United States government to create and maintain conditions under which man and nature can exist in productive harmony." The environmental council and the President are supposed to provide leadership for local communities in disposal, prevention, and so on. But there is no law anywhere to be found in the act. Sentiments only—with a bit of staff and eventually a bit of money thrown in. But no law. No criteria identifying precisely what behavior is thought to be harmful and therefore unlawful. There is not even a small step in this direction. The end result is a new instance of what I call "policy without law." Why indeed should we call such opportunities for discretion "leadership"? It is nothing but governmental impotence. A real commitment to abate pollution would require the setting of clear limits in law on how a person uses his property, whether that property be a factory, a car, or anything else. This takes no leadership, but only choice and courage—and coercion. Leadership in such an area can only mean favoritism, and usually it means favoritism to the worst offenders, because the worst offenders are given subsidies to make slight improvements in their pollution programs. This is not merely inconsistency; it is a new kind of legitimized protection racket.

Antidote for Leadership

It is obviously better not to have any program at all than to give the sense of having one, and later having it revealed as an ineffectual and privilege-prone program that brings the entire governmental apparatus into question. This bears repeating: Chaos is better than a bad program. It is the bad program that gives the sense of a response and then relies on the leadership of agency and clientele groups to make a policy out of the program. No program at all at least provides the opportunity for spontaneous leadership outside the government to propose the more precise and appropriate remedy.

In government, leadership should be classified as one of the ignoble but necessary political arts. Its elevation from the ignoble to the noble has obviously given us little but woe. In government, leadership is just too personal to be relied on. One cannot seek to eliminate the human factor altogether in government, but unless that human factor is narrowly defined within clear and predetermined limits, it is death to legitimacy and therefore to self-govern-ment. Leadership is so different in government because government is not simply one more human endeavor, such as art or business or teaching or science or sports. For the latter endeavors, we want creativity through the almost limitless free play of individual striving. Government is coercion; it is the performance of collec-tive necessities. Therefore it is inevitably gory business and must elevate such boring and ordinary virtues as regularity, predict-ability, and consistency over all the others. These are the essential virtues in government, because without them there is no legitimacy, and unless coercion is seen as legitimate, it becomes raw, brute force, out of which no government can bring a society anything but limitless calamity. In contrast, I have complete faith that desegregation by law will work in the South—as soon as we apply it universally.

The antidote, of course, is law. We speak in the sacred texts and in the high rhetoric of state occasions of government of laws and not of men. But this epigram like all epigrams is as unexamined as it it familiar. Like so many things we learn by rote, it has become a mask for many misconceptions.

Law, first, may need some leadership—just to get itself enacted and perhaps to get itself implemented. But law is basically an alternative to, and to some extent a natural enemy of, leadership. Where leadership is personal, law is ethical; law is made by men but once made it is apart from the men who formulated it and can be judged as good or bad law quite separately from those who made it. In that sense law does reduce, without eliminating, the human factor in government.

Where leadership promotes unity, law promotes separateness. Legislation—that is, a good law, but not necessarily anything drafted by lawyers—is a choice; it categorizes groups, defines jurisdiction, provides benefits, states damages, establishes stand-ards. It declares what is public and what is private—what is subject to government coercion and what is not. This is why I could say leadership in government tends to promote dependence whereas positive law tends to promote independence. For nothing is more rational and individualistic than an ethical statement to the individual that is accessible to his judgment before he acts.

Leaders require followers. Laws require citizens. It is in this sense that the distinguished legal scholar Edward Levi could say that law "is the greatest educational force." Yet law is not the end of politics. A program based on clear legal rules simply transforms the politics to a different plane and mood. The politics of government by leadership and policy without law is a politics of decisions, of who gets what; it is a politics composed of a multiplicity of disputes over the pork barrel. The politics that arises around law is a politics of regulation, of moralities, a dispute over the rules that guide decisions rather than over the specific decisions themselves. Thus, in addition to its education force, the politics of law is far more potentially conflictive than the politics of nonlaw and leadership.

Many on the left of the political spectrum fear and oppose the principle of government by positive law and prefer government by leadership because they associate government of law with conservatism. They parade horrible examples of laws that have protected the upper classes and suppressed the poor. They can remember Supreme Court decisions of the 1930s that knocked down famous New Deal legislation in the name of constitutionality and law. They see laws creating and perpetuating segregation. They are also impressed with social movements and the effectiveness of their leadership in getting radical change.

But similarly, many on the traditional right also prefer the leadership principle because they remember that the Supreme Court was actually overturning some fairly radical legislation by applying, not other laws, but older traditions and practices. Moreover, the right traditionally prefers leadership—or, as they might prefer to call it, authority—and only seeks to replace the present leadership with leaders of its own choosing. Historically, the mark of the conservative regime, be it Louis XIV or Huey I, is the demand to be given the power of governmental leadership so that the "correct" decisions can be made for others.

So, the left carries a preference for leadership in government over from its definition of the requirements of a dynamic society. The right carries a preference for the leadership principle over from its view of authority. Yet note how strongly they agree on the principle itself. Left and right are diametrically opposed on the mere question of whose leaders shall prevail. This is unmistakably true of the various new lefts as well. But this is in no way a profound problem and precisely why neither side has anything profound to say about the current public problems. All sides are operating on misconceptions, and the price is bad government for the rest of us.

On the other hand, the midpoint between the extremes is no solution whatsoever. No compromise between any well-defined extremes is ever fully satisfactory, and it is particularly self-defeating when the extremes are based on silly and false alternatives. Trying to compromise between the present left and right is analogous to mediating a fight between a husband and a wife and having both turn on the mediator.

The way out of this apparent dilemma is to abandon the confrontation altogether and to turn to a new dimension entirely. A pox on both their houses. Both sides have become so bereft of ideas and so dependent on leadership that they possess almost no intellectual responsibility whatsoever. We have nothing to lose by turning to something radically different, even if it is something so quaint as law.

During the more than two centuries of our modern epoch, positive law—legislation—was always the key timber in the edifice of any democratic republic.[5] Whether the goal was one of conserving a certain status quo or establishing a new status quo, the only acceptable mechanism was considered to be a duly enacted positive law, forcefully and by majority processes establishing the desired state of affairs. In any democracy—plebescitary, republican, or bureaucratic—majorities must ultimately overcome minorities. The only effective check against majority tyranny (or any other kind of tyranny) is the requirement that it or its agencies

[5] See Carl J. Friedrich, *Constitutional Government and Democracy*, 4th ed. (Waltham, Mass.: Blaisdell, 1968), esp. chap. 14.

act only through governments duly constituted with laws that citizens can know about clearly before they or the agency enter into the action. The opposite of this state of affairs is what we always meant by the term "arbitrary"; yet we turn to the leadership principle, which can be nothing but arbitrary.

In *The End of Liberalism* I refer to this antileadership system as "juridical democracy." I did not elaborate on it as I should have, because frankly I did not think elaboration was necessary. In our everyday lives we can speak of civility and propriety without defining them at great lengths, because we have some reasonable expectation that we will be understood. It is a measure of the decline of law and legitimate government that I needed more elaboration. This entire volume, but especially this chapter and Chapter 2 was an opportunity to do so.

For those who need also to catalog and classify as well as to understand juridical democracy, it can be said to be susceptible of use by any type of regime. However, it is the only weapon available to those who wish, as I do, to bring about radical transformation of society in order to eliminate injustices. Those who wish to defend the status quo will always have the advantage. Leadership and authority favor them. Interest-group politics favors them. Decentralization favors them. Those who want change must recognize this and more. They must face up to the uncomfortable fact that change must be perpetuated—that the radical must prepare himself to be conservative with respect to his own radical program. A careful evaluation of all possible instruments that might institute a change—rather than pretend to bring it about—will eliminate everything but the juridical principle. Among other things, such an evaluation reveals the ultimate fraud of any revolutionary socialism. Revolution stems from a big bang theory of justice. Eliminate the perpetrators of injustice, and somehow justice is what remains. Revolution, like reaction, is an appeal by leaders for followers. Leadership of a social movement has ultimately only two choices if it seeks to institute its changes, and neither choice is revolution. One choice is to organize the movement into a tightly knit group that can watch over and support its program come what may. This route is the route to conservatism and defense, like the old unions, against whom black newcomers are having to picket. The other choice is law. Group leadership without a government of law is just a new form of feudalism.

On the other hand, protection against radicals is obviously not suppression. Surely the cure would be worse than the disease. The safeguard is an absolute requirement that my government, or any other, say precisely and clearly what it wants before it is allowed to do anything. That is a great preventive for any hare-brained ideas.

No government should be allowed to operate otherwise. The present Establishment, or interest-group liberals, actually believes that if it were not allowed to pass its shoddy programs—if, for example, the Supreme Court declared its broad delegations unconstitutional—chaos would result. I do not believe this; or maybe I just prefer my chaos to their order. Disorder may indeed result from the elimination of many programs. But it seems to me that that is all to the good. If we want a dynamic society we must oppose their notions as well as the notions of the rightwing authoritarians when they cry for law and order. The essence of democratic liberty is not law and order. These are mere claims, from the left and right, to follow their leaders. What we really need is an antidote for leadership, and that antidote is law and disorder.

INDEX